Diary
of a
Taxi Driver

John Lockett would like to thank the following people
for their help with writing this book:

Paul Gray for finding all my old emails
Shell Baker for help and suggestions with my writing
Alison Hendrix for motivating me to write the book
Jim Ireland for being a good friend

Diary
of a
Taxi Driver

John Lockett

BROWN
DOG
BOOKS

Published under licence by Brown Dog Books and
The Self-Publishing Partnership, 7 Green Park Station,
Bath BA1 1JB

www.selfpublishingpartnership.co.uk

ISBN printed book: 978-1-78545-169-0
ISBN e-book: 978-1-78545-170-6

Cover design by Kevin Rylands
Internal design by Andrew Easton
Front cover and maps artwork by Jay Maddison

Printed and bound by CPI Group (UK) Ltd, Croydon CR0 4YY

John Lockett

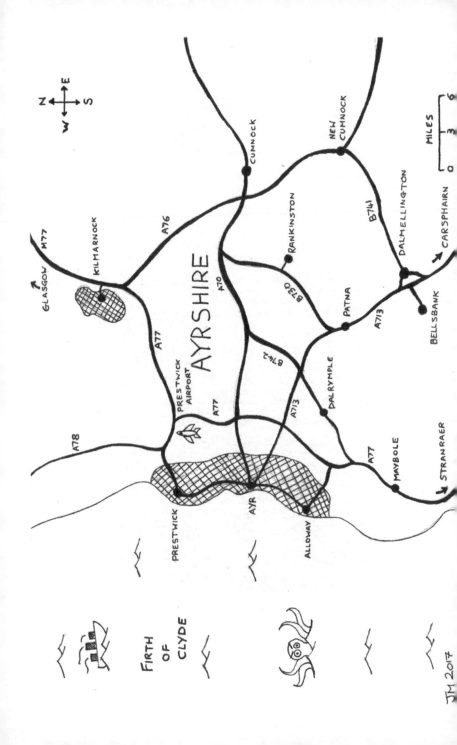

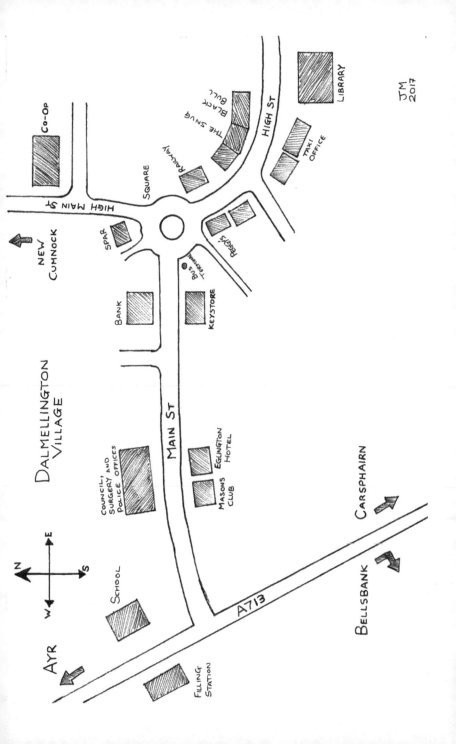

PART ONE – INTRODUCTION

The Driver

My name is John, and for nearly five years from November 2006 to July 2011, I drove a taxi, or more correctly, a private hire vehicle in Ayrshire, Scotland. I was born in 1963 in Birmingham and moved to Dalmellington in 2006 for a variety of reasons. Driving a taxi was originally only a stopgap job. That "stopgap" lasted almost five years. It was a time when I met some truly great people and made some genuine friends. Oh yes, I also had some very interesting encounters which is the whole point of this book. Of the hires I did ninety nine per cent were incident-free and the overwhelming majority of people I met were the nicest folk you could wish to meet.

My previous occupations were nearly all warehousing jobs, driving fork trucks of varying kinds, which I actually enjoyed. Cars never interested me and still don't. I much prefer motorcycles. But when I got the opportunity to learn to drive a car and take my driving test in 1991 I did. I thought it would come in handy one day and I was right. I often got asked to drive company pool cars to places around the country and work off site. The driving didn't interest me at all but seeing new places and meeting new people did.

After I'd moved three hundred miles from where I'd always lived it soon became necessary for me to earn some extra money until my own business started in earnest. I wanted something local so I went to a convenient job centre... i.e. one of the local pubs. I bought a drink and scanned the room. My eyes settled on a guy who looked friendly enough and pretty soon we started up a conversation about this and that and I told him everything about myself and that I was looking for a part time job. He suggested I try the taxi office round the corner, so I finished my squash and went for a very informal job interview with the boss of one of the village's two taxi outfits, the other being run by a chap called Andy. Boss, as I will call him in this book, was a no nonsense kind of guy in his fifties. He ran a private hire business with about three cars, a van of some sort and he needed a driver.

I had a lengthy chat with him and we got on right away. He gave me some pointers and a map of the village to help with my revising for the exam which he arranged for me. A week later I passed my taxi driver test in Kilmarnock. It consisted of getting more than fifteen questions about local streets, routes and landmarks correct out of twenty. I scored seventeen which considering I'd only lived in the village a short while wasn't too bad. I also passed the strict background checks that East Ayrshire Council utilise to weed out unsavoury sorts, and combined with the fact I had a full and clean UK driving licence I soon had my taxi badge and was ready for business.

The accuracy of the following tales is very high. Apart from people's names which I have changed to something like "Fred" or "Mrs B" for obvious reasons, everything else is accurate. Names such as Mr Soanadso or Soandso Street are used where I need to use the name of a person or street without accidentally using another real name or street. All fares are correct at the time the hire occurred.

I emailed these wee stories to my mother within days of them happening so they were fresh in my mind because she liked to hear about all the goings-on. They cheered her up during the last years of her life. One of the reasons I finally stopped driving a taxi was when my mother fell seriously ill back in Birmingham, so I returned to my home town to look after her. Over nearly five years, quite a few stories had accumulated so after polishing the stories up for a wider audience, here they are.

The Taxi

Strictly speaking I drove a private hire vehicle or "minicab" although I took the taxi driver test which entitled me to drive a taxi or PHV (Private Hire Vehicle). A PHV test means you can only drive a PHV not a taxi. Both tests are the same and cost the same. None of that made any sense at the time and it doesn't now to be honest. At the time I drove, the test and badge cost around £150 for three years, and was renewable at the same cost every three years thereafter.

The main (and only apparent) difference between a taxi and a PHV is that taxis can ply for trade and pick up off the street and no name needs to be given to the driver. A person sticks their hand out as they see a taxi approaching, or walks up to one on a taxi rank and gets in and the driver takes them where they want to go.

A PHV cannot ply for trade and pick up off the street. They must be booked in advance, usually via a phone call, or through a regular arrangement and a hirer's name obtained. I believe there are some technical differences too in relation to insurance and MOTs, etc. I never really got bogged down in the minutiae of the job, just the matters that directly affected me. Occasionally, a regular would flag me down like I was a taxi and I would stop and pick them up if I had nothing on at that minute. There was no way I would drive past one of my regulars in the rain.

However if there had been taxis operating in the village, they would doubtless have objected that I had picked fares up off the street, complained to the council and I would have been in some bother or other. But as it was, I never had bother off anyone. The difference between a taxi and PHV to the fare paying customer isn't apparent anyway. Customers would always phone up and ask for a "taxi". In all the years I drove a PHV only one person ever asked for a private hire vehicle, which actually confused me at the time, and they were American. Everyone called our vehicles "taxis"... even the local council.

The Village

Dalmellington and Bellsbank are very hilly communities. Dalmellington was the hub of the village with a bank, surgery, council offices, numerous pubs as well as shops, etc. Bellsbank was an estate or "scheme" at the end of one road to the south with a bar and a few shops. The job was mainly a case of taking senior ladies to the shops or doctors, a few old boys to the old folks' home for tea with their friends or the pub for some booze, and a hectic spate of school kids in the morning and mid-afternoon. There were numerous hires to Prestwick and Glasgow airports too. I enjoyed nearly every hire I had except a handful of incidents you'll read about later.

Boss instructed me in some basics about the village, certain characters I may encounter, rules and various other bits of information including the fact that most of the pubs in the village were known by completely different names to the one on the sign outside. The Railway, Peggy's and The Black Bull were nicknames for the three main pubs in Dalmellington and I quickly committed these important details to memory. The Snug was the only pub in the village that didn't have an alternate name, and doesn't actually feature at all in the following tales. It closed not long after I started too. Boss explained that the alternate names were old ones that the locals still used. Boyd's Bar in Bellsbank had about three old names but for clarity I use only its latest here.

There are about thirty or so roads in Dalmellington and Bellsbank, with one road having an alternate name, one stretch of road having four names and another road having two names with one of those names being almost identical to another road. There was one road that was actually three roads and there was one house that was in a different road to the road in its address. Phew! Isn't town planning wonderful? Within a short space of time I had a map of the village in my head and the job became far easier than the hectic first few days proved to be.

The Office

The taxi office was a motley collection of chairs and a sofa in the waiting area, a wee kitchen and an office which consisted of higgledy piggledy paperwork, a land line phone (which we would divert to a mobile phone if working solo) and the taxi radio. Whoever worked the office radio was known as Control, and the drivers had a radio call sign code of their own and we could all hear each other no matter who was speaking to who.

Boss, radio call sign "TC1", gave me the call sign "TC6" to use on the taxi radio and liked to converse "properly" on it, so it was a case of "Roger" and "over and out" most of the time. There was an unusual occurrence one summer evening in 2007 when I was driving up the brae to Bellsbank, and Natalie, the part-time taxi controller, hailed me on the radio.

Natalie – Control to TC6

Me – Aye, go ahead Control

Natalie – Control to TC6

Me – Yes, I hear you. Go ahead Control

This went on for a few more exchanges with Natalie clearly not hearing my replies. Then more voices came in on the conversation which I could hear, but none of them could hear me.

Natalie – Control to TC6. Where are you?

Me – TC6 here. I've stopped halfway up the Bellsbank brae. What's up, Nat?

Voice 1 – Can you hear a female Scottish voice?

Voice 2 – Yes, I can. Sounds like she's trying to get hold of a "TC6"

Natalie – Hello? Who are you guys?

Voice 1 – We're two radio hams on the south coast of England. Who are you?

Natalie – I can't get hold of my driver. I'm a taxi controller

Voice 1 – Where are you? Scotland?

Natalie – I'm in Ayrshire

Me (wasting my effort) – Hello

Voice 2 – Wow! We're on the south coast of England

Natalie (laughing) – Oh. You haven't heard my driver, have you? Big Brummie bloke by the name of TC6.

Voice 1 (laughing) – No, we haven't, love. We'll let you know if we hear him

Me – Hello, hello, hello. TC6 here

My radio was effectively out for quite a while that night, but the incident never repeated itself. The atmospherics must have played some very strange tricks on the radio signal so I phoned Natalie up from the lay-by I had stopped in. After an hour or so things returned to normal, but the funny thing about the radio signal mix-up was that I could actually see the taxi office radio aerial in my rear view mirror the whole time. The signal couldn't get there, but two guys from five hundred miles away could.

One of the more interesting radio codes that Boss utilised was that if we needed to answer the call of nature, we were to use the code name "Mr Brown" over the radio. We both knew what it meant, but none of our passengers would, and since, unusually, there was no-one in the village with that name, it worked very well for us. It particularly came in useful during the "Great Broken Toilet" fiasco that we endured for a few weeks until a suitable plumber could be located. The office ladies would have to nip to the pub over the road. We would stop at the most convenient pub or the filling station until our office's facilities were restored. Natalie did ask me about it though when I returned from a hire after Boss had announced over the radio that he was going to see "Mr Brown" so he would be out of contact for a few minutes.

Boss – TC1 to TC6

Me – Aye, TC1, go ahead

Boss – I'm off to see "Mr Brown" if you need me. Control, book me out for ten minutes

Me – Roger

Natalie – Roger, TC1

I walked in the office to put the kettle on after this exchange and it went something like this.

Natalie – Oh John, your next hire is in thirty minutes from the Black Bull up to Bellsbank

Me – Aye, OK. Time for a brew then

Natalie (looking at the hire sheet) – Er, John I don't know who this "Mr Brown" is that Boss mentioned on the radio just now. It's not on the booking sheet

Me – Oh that's a "non hire". Not a real person. Don't worry about it

Natalie – Oh so it's like a personal trip in the car somewhere

Me (sniggering) – Aye... yes... personal

Natalie (smiling) – Oh so it's funny is it? Oh go on tell me. What does "Mr Brown" mean? I've got to know

Me – Well, you know the toilet is busted and you have to pop over the road. Well Boss and any other drivers might be elsewhere so we go and see "Mr Brown" at whatever suitable place we can

Natalie (pulling a face) – You mean like behind a hedge?

Me – No we just pop into a pub or the filling station or the council offices. Or we might pop in our own house if it's near. Whichever is more convenient. A hedge. Pffft, you must think we're animals

Natalie – No I just thought... well you know... you blokes...

Me (laughing) – For a trip behind a hedge we'd use the code "Mr Yellow" anyway

Natalie (laughing) – Oh, what are you like?

PART TWO – EVENING SHIFT

Day One – November 2006

After an initial start on day shifts to acclimatise myself with the job, I soon started to work weekend evening shifts. I also did some random day shifts here and there depending on what Boss wanted.

My first ever hire was a disabled guy, and his wife in a wheelchair down to the surgery which I handled far better than Boss (who came along for the ride) expected me to. They were a nice couple who became fairly regular customers of mine, and like a lot of wheelchair users in the village, the lady's chair was easily foldable for placing in the boot. Interestingly enough, after I'd done about three years in the job, every taxi driver in the council area was compelled to attend a course on how to accommodate disabled passengers. In the village I routinely picked up people who were blind or partially sighted or wheelchair users and such like. Every one of them handled their situation differently and I quickly learned how to respond to their needs. The other drivers on the course had similar situations to my own I would imagine, and we all left the day long course thinking a) we learnt nothing of use and b) courses like this should be undertaken before starting the job not after a number of years.

The rest of my first day went pretty well and I was relieved and rather tired after what proved to be quite a busy day. I only had one character who was drunk. I took him a short distance up the scheme from Boyd's Bar and he prattled on the entire trip. I said to Boss after I'd finished my shift that I couldn't understand a word the guy said except the name of the road he lived on.

Boss said that no-one in the village could understand him so that made me feel better about my "ear". Could I understand the locals enough in their accent with my ears being more attuned to a Black Country or Birmingham accent? The answer was "yes", or rather "aye", so that was one issue I didn't have to worry about.

I had already learned local words such as "ken" for "know", "pish" for "nonsense", "blootered" for "drunk", "brae" for "hill" of which there's plenty in the village and "messages" for "grocery shopping" etc. They all seemed to understand me OK too, although one guy thought I sounded Australian.

I only got lost once, and all the hires I had were brilliant. I had to pick up four senior ladies, one after another throughout the village and then take them all to the village hall for some function or other. They were all asking questions and so on. By the time I had picked up my fourth lady, as soon as she got in the car, one of the other three gave her my life story to save me repeating it for the fourth time.

Lady – Och, Mabel. This is John. He's our new driver. He's very nice and he's originally from Birmingham

I think Boss was pleased with me too so I was more than happy with how Day One went.

Day Two – November 2006

It began routinely enough until about two pm when I got a shout over the radio to go and get a guy known as Jab from the Railway pub in the middle of the village and take him home.

I found him with great difficulty due to me not knowing who anyone was and none of them suspecting who this ugly bloke was stood at the door scanning the room, until the barman clicked I was probably the new cabbie that Boss mentioned. After a few weeks, I did think of getting a cap with TAXI on it, but apparently this would have been illegal. I then thought about getting a cap and having T4X1 emblazoned on it, but that would have been illegal also, but by that time most folk knew who I was anyway. My fare was located then staggered out and went to get in the driver's seat.

Me – I think you need the other door, sir

Jab – Sorry, big 'un. Force of habit

Jab relocated to the correct seat and we were soon on our way.

Jab – What time you on 'til?

Me – Five, maybe. Depends on what Boss needs really. I'm easy

Jab – Been busy?

Me – Yeah, busy enough. Only my second day in the job but it's been OK so far

Jab – Aye, you seem right enough big 'un

Jab and the vast majority of my hires over the coming years would nearly always ask the same two standard taxi driver questions at the start of a hire enquiring about my finishing time and busyness.

Me – Why the name Jab? I like nicknames and the story of how people get them

Jab – Cuz I'm a cunt

Me – Er... OK

Jab thrust a fiver in my hand once we arrived at his house.

Jab – I'll give you a fiver pal

I rummaged for change in my cash bag.

Jab – Fuckin keep it son. Your Boss is OK by me

The fare was £2.20p and I thought a £2.80p tip was too much. I didn't want to take advantage of the guy. He was an OK bloke and taking a fiver seemed... you know... wrong. On my second day as well. However I feebly stopped rummaging for change.

Me – A bit overgenerous Jab, but thanks

Jab – I always pay five. Boss will explain

Me – OK Jab

When I caught up with Boss later I asked him to explain Jab's generosity. Most tips I'd had so far were 10p or rounded up a wee bit.

Boss – You see John it's like this. Jab likes a beer and can't get home without us. He tries to keep a fiver spare so he can get home

Me – But he only needs £2.20p to get home

Boss – True enough John, but now and then, very rarely mind you, we take him home for nothing. He REALLY appreciates it. The fivers he's given us in the past as well as being a nice tip, ensure him getting home. A kind of insurance policy. I only have this arrangement with Jab and no-one else so you haven't got to remember a huge list of folks.

In the next few years I took Jab home a handful of times and only once did I take him home for nothing. He was really grateful and far from being a "cunt" as he put it, he was a jolly nice guy.

Settling In - December 2006

On my first evening shift, I had a few ordinary fares until about midnight when I then had to go to pick a lady up from Boyd's Bar. I'd taken her there earlier. I walked in and there were broken glasses and a sticky carpet underfoot with jeering youths everywhere.

Lady – John! He's my new driver

The whole pub heard. At least folk would get to know who I was quick enough, I surmised. She staggered up and told me a few friends were coming back with her.

We all exited to the car park where her bloke urinated profusely over the pub wall. They squeezed into the car with boozy swearing galore and I drove off to a chorus of beery language and yet more swearing. Not at me I hasten to add. I once knew a truck driver back in Birmingham who had the charming nickname of "fuck cunt shit bollocks" because he swore so much.

Her two female mates got dropped off first and I was offered beery lips through the window to kiss. I pecked cheeks so as not to offend and then dropped madam off with her bloke. Later on in the night I dropped an old boy home from the Bowling Club, where they invited me to join, and showered me in Brummie jokes and sandwiches. Great bunch of folks. I left his house and the radio crackled.

Boss – TC6, park up by the church. The fighting outside the Black Bull has got worse

The Black Bull pub was directly opposite the taxi office so we parked up elsewhere to save the cars getting damaged. It was all handbags at ten paces in the end. My first evening shift had ended and I went home tired and slept like a log.

Get Out of the Taxi – December 2006

I had only been in the job a few weeks, and the nearer it got to that first Christmas I'd have done as a cabbie, the more anxious I got to be honest. I'd rapidly learned the streets and a lot of the characters and regulars, but I didn't know as much as I'd have liked. The nearer it got to Christmas, the more people appeared that I didn't know in the various pubs in the village. Works outings and rare get-togethers accounted for a lot of this. Boss took a lot of the customers I wouldn't know, or failing that he tried to describe them, or he'd explain to them that a new driver was picking them up, so he told them to look out for a new face scanning the room for a hire. I don't think many heeded his advice.

On the weekend before that first Christmas in 2006, Boss sent me to Peggy's to get a Mrs Soandso. I can't recall her name now as I never did pick her up.

I arrived at Peggy's in the square and came across a throng of folk outside. It was a mild evening and the night's reverie had moved outside as they drank and danced and laughed. Now I had the task of locating Mrs Soandso. I parked up and got out the car, but before I could lock it up, a young man appeared from nowhere and got in the back seat. No way was he a "Mrs Soandso" who Boss described as the sort of nice lady you'd find working in a bank or something. I reopened my driver's door.

Me – Come on bud, this taxi isn't for you

Bud – Take me up to Bellsbank

Me – No can do mate. I've come for someone else. Sorry

Bud – Take me up to Bellsbank

This was all I needed. I went round to the left side of the car and opened the back door.

Me – Come on mate the taxi is for someone else. Get out please

Bud – Take me up to Bellsbank

He was a right surly individual who was obviously just going to keep repeating "take me up to Bellsbank." I thought, "what the hell do I do now?" and quick as a flash, another youth got in the front passenger seat. "Bollocks," I thought.

Me – Come on lads, for fuck's sake. This taxi isn't for you. It's for a lady, and you two lads are clearly NOT a lady so come on. Get out please

I was actually remaining quite calm and collected considering my predicament. Both of them just repeated their desire to go to Bellsbank. A lady appeared and stood right by me.

Lady – My taxi, I believe

Me – Yes Mrs Soandso, but I'm afraid these two lads have other ideas

Lady – Will you two boys get out of my taxi please?

Bud – No. Take us up to Bellsbank

Now that was enough. I was fuming now. I leant in the car and took the lad in the back seat by the arm and held my face one inch from his.

Me – I'll count to three Sonny Jim, then you'll be out of this car. OK?

Bud – Take us to Bellsbank

Me – One... two... three

I pulled that youth out of there so hard I nearly wrenched my own arm out of its socket. He landed on the pavement and moaned. His mate jumped out the front seat, stepped over Bud on the floor and stood inches away from me. Mrs Soandso quickly climbed in and shut the door. I shut the back door then bounded round to the driver's door and got in the car double quick and hit the door locks. I quickly started the car then slowly pulled away, briefly catching sight of Bud being picked up off the pavement by his mate as I glanced in the rear view mirror.

Me – Sorry about that Mrs Soandso

Lady – Oh I'm not Mrs Soandso, but I could see you needed a hand with those two clowns and were looking for a lady passenger... and I wanted to go home. Boss is a friend of mine and I could see you were having bother. It all worked out nicely I think.

A big smile appeared on my face and I took the lady to her house where she made me a nice cup of tea. I phoned Boss, told him what happened and he went to get Mrs Soandso. When we met up back at the office later he said that Bud and his mate were a pair of herberts who were always getting into bother, but I did the best thing I could have done in getting them out the car. No harm done and a valuable lesson learned.

Not Enough Seats – January 2007

This one Sunday afternoon just after Christmas, I took a nice old boy down to Newton Stewart which is a three-hour round trip so it got me out of the village for a nice change of scenery. I expected the evening to be pandemonium as everybody seemed to want a taxi at the same time to go to some party or other that was announced by someone at the last minute.

I got the shout from Boss to collect some lads from the square and take them up to Bellsbank. Five drunken youths approached the taxi.

Me – I can only carry four of you guys. Come on. You know that

Youth – Och, come on to fuck, it's only up the road. Go on, it's fuckin Christmas

Me – No, and Christmas was days ago anyway

It was swearing galore as they feebly tried to persuade me to carry more than four of them up the road. Eventually four of them got in with the fifth pleading desperately to get in. I drove off with encouragement from the others as they flicked the V sign at him, and left him cold and wet in the rain with his t-shirt clinging to his beer-soaked body. His mates laughed at their friend's unfortunate predicament. No way was I going to risk my licence carrying more than four passengers.

Boss had a wee minibus which could carry eight people, and he sometimes had to use it on regular hires which he would normally do in his car, but for one reason or other he used the minibus. He went to pick some young ladies up in Ayr this one night, and he expected four of them. It went something like this when he told me later.

Girl – Hey Boss, you're in the minibus. How many of us can you take home?

Boss – Eight maximum

Girl – Great, cuz there's six of us altogether

Boss – Get in then

The six piled in.... then three more appeared.

Girl – Hey guys, get in! Boss has brought the minibus

Boss – Ahem. Eight maximum. You now have nine. You can't all get in for fuck's sake

Girl – Oh go on Boss it's...

Boss (butting in) – ... only up the road. Yes, I've heard the script before. One of you needs to get out

They all got out because they didn't want to be split up.

Boss – You lot are unbelievable. You always try and get five in a normal car when we only carry four. This has got room for eight passengers and there's nine of you. There's not enough seats. I'm gonna get a fuckin' Boeing and cut the bastard wings off, but even then you'll find an extra one to cram in. Bollocks to the lot of you

Lassies (en masse) – Oh bollocks to you too!

He returned with no-one.

Drop Off in Rankinston – May 2007

A young lady called Isla who was a regular with us, had booked a hire from Ayr back to the village with two of her mates for one am this particular Saturday night/Sunday morning.

At the appointed hour I arrived at our usual pick up point near Ayr's busy night club area. She and her friends, who I also knew, were already there, together with some blootered young lad I'd never seen before. I pulled up right beside them a few minutes before one am and they all climbed in with the young lad having some difficulty. Seatbelts on, Isla slipped a twenty pound note in my hand and gestured to keep the wee bit of change, and we were off.

Me – Evening ladies... sir. All back to Bellsbank, I take it?

Ladies – Aye... except him

Me – OK where do you want dropping off at sir?

Lad – Rankinston

I was a wee bit annoyed now. Not because twenty pounds was now not enough to cover the seven mile diversion to Rankinston, but I had a hire back in Dalmellington at one thirty am. My one thirty hire was never ready on time anyway so therefore I figured, get this guy home, don't bother asking Isla for the extra on top of the £20, chalk it up to experience and ensure Isla, or anyone else, doesn't drop a diversion on me again.

Me – OK, sir. Bit of a diversion but I can squeeze that in

Lad – Aye. Drop the lassies off first. Then take me to Rankinston

Me – Er. Rankinston is between Ayr and Dalmellington so I'll drop you off on the way, sir

Lad – Look pal, I want you to take the lassies home first...

THEN take me to Rankinston... OK?

I glanced across to Isla who was sat next to me. She looked utterly fed up. I gathered this guy had tagged on to her ride home somehow. I fiddled with my rear view mirror and noticed the two ladies in the back with him not looking too happy either.

Me – OK, sir. I'll see what I can do

Lad – Aye

No way was I going to do the hire in that order. If Isla had specified that route in the first place when she booked it, then fine. But this guy had obviously gate crashed her hire and was now trying to dictate this idiotic route I should do it in.

I pulled off the A713 just before Patna and headed for Rankinston.

Lad – Where you going pal?

Me – Rankinston, sir. To drop you off. I think you must have been under the impression that Dalmellington was nearer than your village when I picked you up. Rankinston first THEN Dalmellington. OK, bud?

Lad – I said I wanted you to...

I could see that the three ladies wanted this herbert out the taxi as soon as possible anyway. The two in the back were squashed up behind me away from him, and Isla looked totally baked off with it all.

Me (butting in) – Matey boy. I'm not interested in what you want. This isn't even your hire. You've crashed it

Lad – We'll see about that

Isla – Oh fuckin shut up. You've scrounged a lift back with us. Just be happy you're getting a free ride home instead of coming the cunt

That was the signal I needed.

Me – I think the sequence of drop offs has been established now, sir. You're getting out next in Rankinston

We swooshed along the B730 and three or so miles later we arrived in the wee village of Rankinston. It was a one road in and out village like Bellsbank and I'd been there before. The lad had moaned and groaned all the way.

Me – Any particular house, bud?

He said nothing, but one of the lassies in the back knew where he lived somehow and pointed to his house. I stopped and he wouldn't move.

Isla – For fuck's sake! Get out man

I got out the taxi and opened the back door on his side.

Me – There you go sir. Thank you for flying Johnny Boy Airlines. Now get the fuck out my taxi!

He got out with a bit of verbal and physical encouragement and I took the relieved ladies back home. I didn't ask how he'd scrounged a lift or how they knew him but I never saw him again, and I tried to make sure I didn't have diversions thrust upon me in the future.

Boobs – July 2007

It was a Friday night and I was sat in the office with Boss. He got a call from a couple needing a taxi into Ayr. Off I went, picking them up from the square in the centre of Dalmellington and we were soon off down the A713. They were friends of one of our regulars, Boss informed me, so I didn't expect any nonsense.

The bloke got in behind me. His missus was totally blootered and fell across his lap as soon as she managed to pour herself in through the back door. They were a regular looking couple in their thirties. So, after the usual questions about my busyness and finishing time were all nicely dealt with came a question that shocked even me.

Bloke – My wife is having a boob job. What do you think about that?

Me – Fine

That became my standard answer to a lot of pish I got asked in the following years.

Bloke – I think she needs bigger boobs. What do you think?

Me – Er... Not really my place to comment, sir. I'm just a humble taxi driver

Bloke – Oh go on. Tell me if you think my wife needs a boob job

This is a very heavily shortened version of this little exchange but basically this guy wanted me to ogle his wife's boobs and comment on them. No way would this happen whether she was drunk, or sober as a judge.

Now then, at this point I wasn't even past a wee village called Waterside. Still ten miles or more to go before I got to Ayr. No amount of stalling and avoiding the question was going to get me out of this one. He just kept on and on and on.

Me – Well, what does your wife think?

Bloke – Ah she's blootered anyway. She wants one though. Don't you, love?

She slurred something which I couldn't decipher.

Me – Well, I'll have a look once we get to Ayr

A lie obviously, just to shut the guy up. The rest of the journey into Ayr passed fairly quietly with the two of them snogging and what not. We arrived in Ayr after what seemed an age.

Me – Where in Ayr do you need, sir?

Bloke – Miller Road, pal

I knew Miller Road well so I headed there and was glad that the subject of his wife's boobs seemed to have been forgotten. Driving down the last bit of the A713 before Morrisons, his wife blurted out she wanted me to stop. Now at this point I thought, "Oh no. She wants me to check her boobs out now! I'm doomed." But she opened the door and spewed on the pavement with her hands on the kerb leaning and lurching out the car.

Bloke – Sorry about that pal. I'll go round and see if she's OK

Me (looking round) – No need to be sorry, sir. No spew in the car from what I can see. I just hope your missus is OK

He got out, went round her side and with a wee bit more spew out the way, she was soon back in and we were on our way. We got to Miller Road and she got out and spewed once again over the pavement.

Missus – I don't feel well. Can we go home?

Bloke – We'd best

Me – Aye… Where's home, sir?

Bloke – Other Street, Prestwick

So they got back in and we were off to Prestwick, which is a town that joins the north of Ayr and their street was at the very southern end, so it was only a few miles up the road. Apart from that I actually wanted to get the lady home rather than have her being ill away from it.

We were one corner away from their road, when the guy mentioned boobs again, only to be foiled by his missus shouting for me to stop again for another wee spew. We finally arrived at their house. The journey seemed to last forever and I eased the handbrake on.

Me – £21.90p please, sir

I then waited for him to ask me to check out his wife's boobs. Thankfully I was saved by his missus rushing out the car, spewing some more, and up their path towards the house.

Me – I hope your wife is better soon, sir. She doesn't seem very well at all

He apologised for all the messing about and gave me £25 and told me to keep the change which meant a nice tip for me. If she hadn't spewed so much I really do think he would have actually got out his wife's boobs for me to check.

Shh - October 2007

I picked up Mrs R from Boyd's Bar in Bellsbank late one Friday night. I think I saw no-one else as I drove up to collect her. She swayed gently as I approached Boyd's but got in the car easily enough. She wanted Main Street, Dalmellington. Total distance of about a mile, if that. So off we go, and I knew the lady well even though this was the first time she'd been in my taxi. She worked in one of the shops in the village. As I was driving down the brae between Bellsbank and Dalmellington, I asked her destination.

Me – Where to in Main Street, Mrs R?

She put her finger to her lips.

Mrs R – Shh!

Me – No-one will hear us Mrs R. Where do you want to go?

By now I had turned into Main Street and was crawling along the road.

Mrs R – Shh. I don't want to go home

So there was now the possibility that I was lumbered with her in my taxi all night unless I knew where she lived ... and didn't take her there.

Me (whispering) – Where is home Mrs R, so I don't accidentally take you there?

By now I was coming to a halt.

Mrs R (pointing) – There

She pointed to the flat directly above the shop I'd just stopped outside. What were the chances? So I eased the clutch back out and crawled along some more. A wee bit further on she signalled me to stop. A bit more "Shh" while she paid me then she staggered out. I made sure she went in one of the nearby doorways rather than pulling away and leaving her alone or possibly falling over. She noisily entered a doorway and I quietly pulled away. Job done and I never had her in the taxi again.

Dump the Chips Love – October 2007

I went to Ayr one Saturday night to pick up one of our regulars, George. A nice guy he was, in his late twenties maybe, and I was looking forward to a nice chat on the way back to the village. I parked in our usual pick up spot and waited. Boss was parked behind me in his taxi picking up someone else.

 I saw George walking to the car on his own and thought, "Great, he's on time. Get him home then I'm finished... and home to bed." I popped the door lock to let him in.

George – Hi John, I'll just get the missus and her mate who's coming back with us. They've gone for chips

At this point I should mention that eating in the taxi was not allowed. Not by Boss or East Ayrshire Council. I sometimes let a sober regular eat, but not a sloppy curry of "messy" food and only if I reckoned we wouldn't get spotted and they weren't blootered.

Boss (over the radio) – Where's George going?

Me – To find his missus and her mate

Boss – Well if they've got food tell them they're not getting in the taxi. I've just had them valeted

Me – No problem

George promptly returned with his drunken missus and her equally drunken mate and they were both laden with curry and chips slopping everywhere. I'd never seen either of them before as I always picked George up on his own or with a few of his buddies. He got in the back seat.

Me – George. I can't let your missus and her mate in here with food. Boss is right behind us and anyway they're blootered and will get it everywhere and make a right old mess

George – Aye, you're right

Me – And I can't afford the time to hang around waiting for them to scoff it either. I've got a hire back in the village in thirty minutes so time is tight as it is

I wound the passenger window down an inch to converse with Mrs George and hit the door locks.

Me – Sorry, but you can't bring those chips in here

Mrs George (I never knew her name) – Why?

Me – a) You're blootered. b) You'll get it everywhere. c) Boss is parked behind us and d) There's police and taxi marshals everywhere. It isn't happening

Mrs George – For fuck's sake! We use Boss's taxis all the fuckin' time and this is the service we get!

George – Come on, love. Dump the fuckin' chips and let's get home. John's right. It's Boss's taxi and he doesn't want it messed up and with the police everywhere he'll get busted

Mrs George's mate walked back to Boss's taxi and I watched her argue with him in my rear view mirror. Boss just gave her the old head shake routine and she started to lose it. I could hear her ranting and raving over the noise of Ayr on a Saturday night.

Boss (over the radio) – They've got ten seconds to ditch the food and then you pull off with whoever is in the car. Sorry about this George but I'm not having it. Ten... nine... eight

George (I cued the radio mic for him) – Aye, you're right enough, Boss

Mrs George continued to demand I unlock the door so she could get in. The car wobbled as she tugged on the door handle. She was absolutely livid.

George – For fuck's sake, love! Dump the chips and get in the bastard taxi. John will pull off without you. Believe me

Boss (over the radio) – Three... two... one

Neither Mrs George nor her mate were going to dump their beloved chips and curry. A lot of it they'd accidentally dropped on the pavement anyway with all their gesticulating.

Boss (over the radio) – Zero. TC6, off you go

Me – Well, George, I'm pulling out. Are you with me or getting out?

George – Take me home

I pulled away and I witnessed Mrs George and her mate jump up and down dropping chips all over the place as I looked in the rear view mirror. So rather than my usual nice chat with George I had to listen to him argue on his mobile with his missus for the entire journey.

The Man Who Cried – December 2007

Boss gave me a hire one evening after midnight to take a young lass of about twenty and her chap down to Ayr. It was late on a cold Saturday evening and once I had dropped them off I was finished for the evening so I looked forward to a nice pleasant trip down the deserted A713 followed by home then bed. I picked them up from a house in Dalmellington and we were soon on our way. She was a bright and breezy chatty young lass while he looked a bit fed up.

The lass talked more than me which is saying something, but I liked the conversation and it made the journey more pleasant. We talked about nothing of importance or note, but her chap started to show signs of irritation and told her to be quiet.

She ignored him and carried on chatting to me but I decided to keep my end of the conversation to as few words as possible in an attempt to kill it really. He started getting a bit arsy after a while and told her to shut up very firmly.

Chap – Oh shut up, love!

Me – You OK back there, mate?

Chap – No. My missus is trying to chat you up and I'm fed up with it

Lass – I am not trying to chat the driver up. Don't be so childish. We're just having a nice chat, aren't we driver?

Me – Yes. But I think I should pay more attention to the road now. Some sheep got out along the fence here the other week and... well, you can imagine

I made up the story about the escaped sheep and stopped talking. I negotiated a slight bend in the road between Hollybush and the outskirts of Ayr. Suddenly the chap in the back cried out.

Chap – What you doing, driver? Going a bit fast aren't you for these bends?

Me – Sir, I can assure you I know how to drive and I'm well in control

I adjusted my rear view mirror a wee bit. He was sat directly behind me. I came to another very slight bend in the road and I glanced in the mirror as he deliberately smacked his head hard against the door window.

Chap – Ouch! Watch it driver!

A lay-by was about a hundred yards ahead which I immediately planned for. I braked heavily and swung into it. The car scattered a few bits of loose gravel here and there as we ground to a halt. Seatbelt already off, I applied the handbrake and swiftly exited the car. I opened the rear door next to Chap.

Me – You and me need a man to man chat out here. Come on.

He meekly got out and immediately started crying. "Bloody

hell," I thought. I took a few steps and moved round to the back of the car and he followed.

Me (quietly) – I don't know what your game is here mate but I'm not very happy at all with you smacking your head against the window and trying to blame it on my poor driving

Chap (blubbing) – I'm sorry pal, but I thought you were trying to chat my girlfriend up

Me – Well, I can assure you I'm not. I'm forty-odd years old and got a girlfriend at home waiting for me when I get back from this hire. Sorry if you've got the wrong end of a stick here, chap

I gave him a friendly slap on the shoulder.

Me – Are we OK here now, chap? I want to get home and... well you know... my girlfriend is lying in bed all warm... catch my drift?

He quickly got it together and the rest of the journey passed without further incident or indeed, conversation. I did however wish I had a girlfriend back at home, although she would have been well asleep by the time I returned home at stupid o'clock.

Aggressive Youth – January 2008

It was about two am on the 3rd of January 2008, and I'd just come out of Boyd's Bar picking up Rachel. She became one of my regulars. She was a lady in her late forties you do not mess with. I stepped out the pub, while she stayed back to finish her drink and say goodbye to her friends, and walked past a local herbert in his early twenties, who I knew. I'd seen him on the way in and thought nothing of it. He was just hanging about waiting for friends, I imagined.

Youth – Who's the taxi for pal?

Me (in a jokey fashion) – Well, that's for me to know and you not to know

I thought he might appreciate a wee joke but I was wrong.

Youth – You cheeky, fuckin' cunt

He staggered towards me as I opened the driver's door. I got in sharpish and thought... "I'm getting out of his way." He promptly stood by the car door and tried to punch me... and punched the side window, which was wound up due to it being freezing cold weather. He backed off moaning and groaning and rubbed his hand which must have hurt like hell, the force he punched with. I wound the window down a wee bit. I was going to make a comment but Rachel suddenly appeared at the pub door. The youth clearly didn't realise that she was getting in my taxi.

Rachel – What the fuck you doing?

Youth – I tried to punch that cheeky fuckin taxi driver but the window was up

Rachel – You silly, wee cunt. Fuck off. He's my taxi driver

She gave him a slap on the head for good measure and he cleared off.

Peas – February 2008

Sundays were normally a fairly quiet affair. There was a wee rush in the morning when I ferried two or three car loads of senior ladies up the church, a few regulars to and from old folks homes, and drunks back to their own house from whichever house they'd woke up in that morning. Some of them had to look outside the house and give me landmarks so I could work out where they were because they had no idea.

Then there was normally a lull until late afternoon/early evening when I then ferried the collection of old boys home who had spent all day doing some serious hard drinking in Dalmellington's various establishments. It was the usual Sunday fare, and I got used to it pretty quickly.

I could virtually predict when the phone would ring and who it would be, and this one Sunday was a carbon copy of the previous dozen or so. I was expecting another quiet evening, loafing about on the luxurious sofa in our well appointed office playing the amazing mobile phone game, Gem Drop, the best time killer known to mankind. I got a call about six pm to pick up Tom from Peggy's and take him home. Not a problem I thought. A likeable old guy as the vast majority of folk were to be honest. I found him easily enough swigging the last few drops of his beer.

Me – Hi Tom! Let me get you home

Tom – OK, John. Now watch these fuckin' peas

He pointed at a wee bit of crumpled tinfoil on the table.

Me – Peas, Tom? Why have you got peas in the pub? It looks like a lump of tinfoil to me

Tom – Well, they're peas and I don't want them getting damaged

I looked round the pub a wee bit confused. The barmaid nodded at me and mouthed the word "peas" so I reckoned... yeah... peas... OK, I'm cool with that. I picked up the wee tinfoil bag because Tom needed both hands to navigate his way out the pub, across the pavement and into the taxi. I could feel a bit of warmth through the tinfoil. Apparently they were home grown by someone in the village and Tom loved them. The barmaid had a handful spare so she warmed them for him to take home. This was the sort of stuff I loved.

Hooker – February 2008

Boss gave me my last hire of the night at midnight this one Sunday to run four young lassies into Ayr. I knew them pretty well. They spent the drive into Ayr talking about which blokes they were going to shag and that one of the other taxis in the village smelled of fanny. Apparently the driver had a lass and two guys in it the other day and "things went on". So after this little episode, I drove back to Dalmellington knowing I had finished and would soon be heading home.

I got back to the office, and there was a young lady hanging about. I had never seen her before so I just headed for the office door using my best avoidance technique but she spotted me.

Lass – Are any of these pubs open?

Me – No. They all shut at midnight. It's one am now so you won't get in any of them. If they've got a "lock in" you're knackered really

Lass – Fuck. I'm looking for my boyfriend. He's in one of these pubs but I don't ken which one

From the front door of our taxi office you could see four pubs. The furthest was about forty yards away.

Me – Oh. Er. I'm afraid I can't help you, love

Lass – Does Boss still run this taxi place?

Me – He does. You know Boss then?

Lass – Aye. I'm freezing. Can I come in and warm up?

Me – I'll ask Boss. We're finished now. What's your name?

She told me her name. She wasn't blootered but she had hardly anything on and looked froze to death. I asked Boss and he said she's OK so I let her in the office. Her and Boss proceeded to chat about this and that and I quickly deduced he'd known her a while. I counted my money and cashed in. Boss then paid me my wages and I was ready for home.

Me – When do you need me next Boss?

Boss – Thursday, nine, am. I got some stuff to do and you can cover for me

Me – Aye, OK

Lass – I'll come out with you

I thought at this point nothing was unusual. Perhaps she was going to try to find her bloke now. As we came out the door, the Black Bull was finally throwing out its "late drinkers". If they wanted a taxi now it was tough, but they usually lived just up the road.

Me – Perhaps your bloke is in there. Go and ask before the door gets shut

She asked and her bloke wasn't there, and there was no-one left inside either.

Me – Well, he must be in the Railway or Peggy's then. The Snug is already shut

Lass – Fuck it

I started my car and proceeded to scrape my windscreen to remove a wee bit of frost.

Lass – Where you going?

Me – Home

Lass – Back to your wife, I suppose. Girlfriend, maybe?

Me – No, I'm single at the moment

Lass – I'll come back to yours with you. We can have a good time

Where did that come from? I could see Boss out the corner of my eye as I suddenly sped up my ice scraping routine. He'd come out for a spot of freezing cold night air. He slowly shook his head.

Me – I'm knackered, love. I've just finished a fourteen-hour shift

I wanted out of there. She was quite a pretty lass actually. Slim, about twenty-five years old but I just wanted my bed.

Lass – Well, let's go down that alley for ten minutes

Now this was ridiculous!! I remember once many moons ago in the early 1980s a lass dragged me back to her place for repulsive acts, but at least I'd known her longer than five minutes! And we didn't go up the side of the Bull either!

Me – Er... I really want to get home, sweety. Maybe if you're in Dalmellington again sometime?

Lass – OK

I scraped the last bits of ice off my windscreen sharpish and trundled home. When I got into work on the Thursday, Boss was having a wee chuckle to himself.

Me – Morning, Boss

Boss – Aye, morning, John

Me – You seem rather jolly. What's up? You farted or something?

Boss – No laddie. I was just thinking how nicely you avoided that lass on Sunday night. You saw me shake my head, I assume?

Me – Aye, but I didn't take it as a warning. I just thought you were giving the situation a kind of "oh deary me"

Boss – Well... I've known her years and she's done stuff like that before. She saw you getting paid and thought "I want some of that"

Me – Aha! Not my good looks or charm then?

Boss – No, John... No

Me – She wanted some cash

Boss – Aye. She'd have some cash and you have a fiddle about in her knickers if you ken what I mean

Me – I know what you mean, Boss... Pretty lass though

Boss – Aye she's a pretty enough lassie. But you're better off keeping your cock in your pants

Me – Aye right enough, Boss

Metal To Maybole – March 2008

Natalie passed a hire to me early one Saturday evening to take four local lads down to Maybole. They were all about eighteen I guessed, but not regular taxi users so I never remembered their names even though I saw them around the village most weekends. I picked them up from the square and we were soon off down the A713 at regulation speed while I listened to a Pantera CD in the stereo. The lads chatted amongst themselves about this and that, but as they got louder I turned my CD up more. I needed some metal instead of their pish talk. A lull in their conversation changed the whole journey. The lad in the front seat spoke.

Lad – What the fuck is that, man?

Me – What's what?

Lad – That noise coming out the radio

Me – That "noise" is Pantera, and it's a CD not the radio

Lad – It's fuckin' awesome, pal!

Me – Oh you like it then?

Lad – This is fuckin' unbelievable. I have never heard music like this ever. Feel the fuckin power, man!

One lad was totally freaking out in the back left seat, hanging out the window and shouting his head off at all the sheep in nearby fields. The lad in the middle pulled him back in. The lad behind me just looked amazed by it all and the lad in the front seat wanted it louder.

Lad – Fuckin' turn it up man!

Me (turning the volume up) – OK lads. Wow, I honestly didn't think you lot would like metal

Lad – Metal?

Me – Yeah metal. Heavy metal or whatever you want to call it

Lad – This is metal? Wow. It's fuckin' brilliant

One of the lads in the back shouted that this was the greatest music he'd ever heard.

Lad – Drive faster John

Me – OK

I dropped the car down to fourth gear, accelerated very briefly, then slipped it back into top and settled at exactly the same speed I was driving at before. It was a trick I'd learned for when someone tried to hurry me up.

I had never in all my life met anyone, never mind four people at once, listen to metal for the first time and be instantly converted. We got to Maybole and they were exhausted after thrashing about in the car so much.

The one lad loved the music so much, I gave him the CD. It was a burned copy I'd made of Pantera's Reinventing the Steel album, and I was always glad to spread the "word" as it were. I gave a few CDs away to various folks over the years, but I'd never had lads like that in the car at the same time.

The Day I Quit – March 2008

Obviously there are some tiresome and awkward punters from time to time. Some got a bit mouthy, and it was hard work ignoring all the nonsense and abuse while keeping a civil tongue in my head sometimes. Usually I only got around one incident a month. The longest you would have to endure it would be thirty minutes which was a run to or from Ayr. I'd been in the job about sixteen months working weekend evenings plus the odd shift here and there, then a tsunami of nonsense all converged into one big Super Saturday of incidents that pushed me to the limit.

After a fairly busy start with all the usual punters I went to pick up three young ladies from an address in Burnton, a wee community just to the north of Dalmellington. Boss picked up another three from the same address a few minutes behind me. I only recognised the one lass who got in my car, but off we went to the Railway pub which was their destination of choice for that evening.

Me – Railway then, ladies?

Always best to check in case they changed their mind.

Lass 1– No. We're going to the Dalmellington Inn

Me – Same pub. A lot of pubs round here have got more than one name. An official name and a kind of nickname

Lass 1 – Sounds odd

Me – Confused me when I started this job

Lass 3 (the local) – Aye, that's right

Boss came over the radio.

Boss (radio) – TC6, your next hire is from *inaudible* where you're dropping those lassies off

Me (radio) – TC1, these lassies say they're going to the Railway

Pandemonium ensued as I tried to listen to Boss on the radio over the hysterical cackle of half-blootered women.

Me (radio) – Er TC1, is that the Railway you said there?

Boss now ranted and raved for a while. I couldn't make him out over the screaming in my cab and the screaming in his cab. I desperately tried to quieten my ladies down.

Me – Ladies, please. Can I have a bit of hush? I can't hear my boss on the radio

Lass 2 – Turn the fuckin radio up then

Me – It's flat out now

Lass 1 fiddled with the radio/CD player.

Me – Er.. wrong radio, love. I'm talking about the taxi radio

Lass 3 was the local girl and she just kept shouting "Railway! Railway!" Anyway they quietened down a wee bit.

Me (radio) – Er, TC1 I had some bad reception there. What did you say the drop off address was again?

Boss (radio, shouting at the top of his voice) – New Street!

The address he gave me was not the Railway, but a house in the next street. By now I was totally brassed off and going deaf with the constant ranting and raving from Boss over the radio and the ladies in my car.

Lass 3 – No we're not. We're going to the Railway. The fuckin' Railway

Me (to no-one in particular) – For fuck's sake!

Lass 1 – Fuck off yourself

Me (stopping the car) – Don't tell me to fuck off

Lass 2 – You told us to fuck off

Me – I said "for fuck's sake". Exasperation you know. We're having a performance sorting out where you're going

Lass 3 – The fuckin' Railway

Me – Jeezo

Lass 1 – We're not from round here. We're from Cumnock

Me – Oh, nice

Lass 2 – Yeah sorry, pal

Me – Ladies, I'll take you to the Railway. Let's all relax, eh?

I just drove off to the Railway, but as I entered the square...

Lass 1 – Ooh, I need the bank. Can we go to a cashpoint instead?

Me (through gritted teeth) – Certainly, ladies

So I dropped them off at the bank which is nowhere near the Railway pub. I radioed Boss and told him where I'd dropped them. I expected him to send me to New Street to do the next pick up... but he sent me somewhere completely different and he did the New Street hire. So all that arguing and earache was a complete waste of time. I was a wee bit irate at this point. A load of old nonsense and abuse for nothing.

I did a few more hires over the next hour or so, then I found some fags and driving licence kicking about in the passenger foot well that someone had dropped. I radioed Boss and told him I'd drop into Boyd's Bar in Bellsbank to return some lost property next time I was passing.

It must have been a big night or a party or something because Boyd's Bar was heaving when I popped in there a short while later. Everyone was blootered and the place was packed. I went for a walk round the pub to see if I could find the owner of the fags and driving licence. I'd dropped them off there about thirty minutes before. One lad kept trying to trip me up. An extremely drunk senior lady tried to snog me the entire time as she clung on and followed me round. Then another lad wanted to wrestle me. The problem was I knew them all and they thought it was hilarious. I was absolutely fuming now and I couldn't even find the person I was looking for. I gave up and headed back to the office.

After a quiet spell when everyone was in the pub of their choice, Boss and myself met back at the office to microwave some coffee, talk some pish and I also handed the lost fags and driving licence to him. Now at around eleven fifty-five pm every Saturday one of us headed off to pick up two guys from a pub in Prestwick. Boss or myself picked them up every week from the same pub at the same time. Never any hassle. They were great guys and I always got a nice tip if I got the shout rather than Boss doing it himself. The time approached eleven fifty-five pm.

Boss – John, go and do the Colin and Paul hire. And if their fuckin' mate from Alloway wants to hitch a ride you haven't got time. You've got to be back in Ayr for 1.30 am to get Mrs B from her usual pick up place OK? So no diversions. Tell him to get to fuck

Me – No problem

The plan was therefore to arrive at Prestwick at twelve-thirty am, get Colin and Paul, bring them back to Dalmellington, then go back to Ayr for Mrs B at one-thirty am. I'd done this particular series of runs a couple of times by now so I looked forward to a peaceful end to a stressful evening. I drove over to Prestwick which around midnight was a straightforward drive with zero traffic down the A713. I pulled up outside the pub and an obviously drunken woman sprinted over the road towards me.

Her – Take me to fuckin' Kilmarnock

Me – Sorry love, I can't. I'm booked

Her – Who?

Me – Two of my regulars. I get them every week

Her – Fuck 'em

Me – They ain't that pretty, love... Listen if they ain't there I'll see you in a minute. OK?

Her – Fuck off

She quickly deduced that there was no way I would take her to Kilmarnock and she cleared off screaming at the next taxi or private hire she could find, but it was yet more annoyance on top of the previous load I'd endured.

I slipped in the pub, found Colin and Paul and noticed two other guys with them. One of them was a mate of theirs called Bill who I'd dropped off a few times in the past, but he lived on the route back so if he wanted to tag along that wouldn't mean diverting and he was a decent chap anyway. I didn't know who the fourth guy was but I had this horrible feeling it was "Mr Alloway" and he'd want me to take him home.

Me – Evening, gentlemen. I'll go and sit in the car. I managed to park right outside tonight instead of the usual half a mile up the road

Paul – John, can you drop our mate off in Alloway?

I thought to myself, "I just knew it. I just knew it. It is Mr

Alloway." I looked at my watch.

Me – Sorry Paul, sorry sir, but I'm on a really tight schedule tonight

Paul – OK, no problem

Mr Alloway – mmmmfffftttt

Me – Queen Margaret Academy roundabout on the bypass is the best I can do I'm afraid

Mr Alloway – mmmmfffftttt

I left and sat back in the car and within a few minutes the four of them emerged from the pub and got in with Colin sitting in front. I thought, "I hope this herbert doesn't expect me to take him to Alloway." Bill got dropped off first in Prestwick itself, then I set off to drop Mr Alloway at the roundabout, then I could head back to Dalmellington.

Mr Alloway – Are you taking me home then, driver?

Me – Er…

Colin – He can't, he hasn't got time. He'll drop you at the roundabout

Mr Alloway – For fuck's sake. I can't walk all that way. Fuckin take me home pal

Now I was absolutely fuming, and pissed off.

Me – Er, I ain't got time, mate. I did mention it in the pub. You got in here knowing that. As far as I'm concerned you can either get out at the Queen Margaret Academy roundabout or come back to Dalmellington with us. You made the decision to get in here

Mr Alloway – You cunt

Me – Oh am I?

Paul – John did explain in the pub. He hasn't got time

Me – I'm not stuck in a taxi not going where I want it to. I can't be a cunt

Colin – Be reasonable. John told us before you got in he can't take you

Me – Your call, bud

I would under normal circumstances never have been that cheeky to anyone, but I was totally brassed off by this point and Mr Alloway let himself get into this situation on his own. Colin and Paul were really nice chaps, but I had no time for their mate whatsoever. I could tell that Colin was really uncomfortable with the whole situation.

Mr Alloway just kept on and on and on though and I finally cracked. I didn't want to take him home at all but the choices I had were to sit in the car at the roundabout waiting for him to get out... which he probably wouldn't, or drive back to Dalmellington with him ranting and raving in the back seat the whole journey.

Me – You want Alloway yes?

Mr Alloway – Yes, pal

Me – O fuckin' K then

So I took him home as fast as the car would safely allow, deliberately skidding to a halt outside his house.

Me – There you go, sir

Mr Alloway – Cheers, pal

Me – Don't fuckin' "pal" me, and you'll never get in a taxi if I'm driving it ever again. Understand?

Mr Alloway just looked at me as I pulled off and headed back to the village at a brisk pace with Colin and Paul attempting light hearted chit-chat to alleviate the obvious tension. I dropped them both off in Dalmellington at their respective abodes, with Colin giving me an extra fiver for the bother, and headed back to Ayr for Mrs B after a quick exchange with Boss on the radio.

Me – TC6 returning to Ayr to get my next hire

Boss – Roger, TC6. Mr Alloway with your last hire was he?

Me – Aye, he was

Boss – How did you get on with him?

Me – He's off my Christmas card list Boss

Boss – Is he now? Well I'll tell you something. He's Colin's brother

Me – Is he?

Boss – Aye. I'll chat with you later back at the office to get the full scoop, but I imagine I'll be having a wee chat with Colin about him in the week

Me – Righto Boss. Leaving the village now. Over and out

Boss – Roger

I was ten minutes late setting off for Mrs B which wasn't too bad I suppose but I prided myself on being on time for every hire. It was just yet more annoyance and I came to the decision on that drive to Ayr that I wasn't going to work another late shift unless Boss was desperate. I didn't like to let Boss down. I liked the guy.

Mrs B was the usual nice pleasant hire after I picked her up just a few minutes late, then I finished off the evening with the awfully decent Mr M back down to Ayr and I got back to base around three am. Finished. I was going to tell Boss then that I'd do days and weekend days, but no more weekend evenings, but a mate of his had popped round the office, so I cleared off home to bed.

I told him the next day and he was OK about it but said he hadn't enough work for me on just days so we'd have to part company. We shook hands and that was that. I gathered up my stuff from the office and taxi which consisted of a chipped tea mug, a dog eared paperback or two, a wee bag crammed with rock and metal CDs and a street map of all the villages in Ayrshire with the covers hanging off. I drove home thinking, "I suppose I'd better find a job tomorrow then."

My mobile rang two days later and it was Boss. We had a good long chat and came to an arrangement. I was a taxi driver again although working different hours and shifts to before.

PART THREE – DAY SHIFT

Mr Who? – April 2008

I was driving a taxi again on day shifts with an occasional evening, so I thought there would probably be less scope for adventures and sundry nonsense to occur. How wrong I was. There was obviously less abuse, threats of violence and all the reasons I quit in the first place, but the day shift still had scope to astonish and amaze.

Friday daytime about four pm and I'd just finished a few hires and was returning back to the office, so I could warm my coffee up once more in "Old Sparky" the microwave. As the street outside the taxi office was packed with parked cars I parked on the opposite side of the street outside the Black Bull.

I pulled up, turned the ignition off and I noticed Mr H, the Bull's barman stood outside having a smoke. He gestured at me. I wound the passenger window down so I could hear him.

Me – Hi, Mr H. How you doing?

Mr H (pointing over the road) – John. Can you take that chap home?

Over the road was a senior gentleman tottering about outside our taxi office. I was working alone this particular day so I kept the office locked while I was out. I recognised the guy as being a village local but didn't know who he was. He always used Andy's taxis, so consequently I didn't know some crucial information about him. i.e. where he lived or his name. If I could get the guy home though, Boss would doubtless know who he was, and I would effectively have "stolen" one of Andy's customers. Boss loved that, and I'd never managed to steal one yet.

Me – Sure, Mr H

By this time, the old boy had bobbled over the road towards my taxi, Mr H opened the passenger door for him and he plonked himself in the front seat.

Me – Where do you want to go, sir?

Bloke – azz azz azz burp, big 'un, burp azz

Me – Sorry, sir. I didn't quite catch that.

Bloke – azz azz burp azz burp big 'un azz burp

Me – Mr H, I can't understand a word this guy says. Do you know where he lives?

Mr H – I think he lives in Soandso Street

Me – Soandso Street has got over fifty houses in it. What chance have I got?

Bloke – azz burp, big 'un, brap azz 35 brap azz burp azz

I actually managed to pick out number 35 but I know he didn't live there because one of my regulars did. At this point I didn't care about what the guy's name was. I just wanted to get him home.

Mr H – There you go. Number 35 Soandso Street

Me – He can't live there. I know who lives there and it isn't this guy

Mr H gave me a helpful shrug of the shoulders as if to say, "Well, he's in your taxi now. Your problem." I pulled away, turned round in the wee car park and headed for Soandso Street figuring that at some juncture he would point to his house.

Bloke – burp azz azz, big 'un, brap azz burp, etc, etc, etc

He just went on and on and on, all the while playing with three fivers in his hand.
  I arrived in Soandso Street and glanced over to the guy who was scanning the houses as I crept along. Hopefully he'd point or say something. It was a cul-de-sac so I turned round at the end and crawled back the way I'd come.

Bloke – azz azz burp, big 'un,azz brap burp number 55

Aha! I heard number 55 in there so I was immediately much happier and I pulled up outside 55 Soandso Street.

Me – There we are, sir. Home safe and sound

Bloke – brap azz what burp azz brap burp the fuck azz burp azz azz are we doing azz azz brap here?

Now I picked out, "What the fuck we doing here?"

Me – Mr H said you lived in Soandso Street

Bloke – burp burp azz azz Otherway Road burp azz azz, big 'un

Me – Aha! Have you there in a jiffy, sir

Luckily I hadn't gone in completely the wrong direction because Soandso and Otherway are very close to each other. I arrived at his house in about one minute and heaved a sigh of relief. All the while I'd been driving, the old boy had been rummaging around in his pockets. The three fivers were transferred from hand to hand as he went through every pocket in his trousers, jacket and lord knows what else.

Me – I've got change if you need it, sir

Finally after much rummaging, accompanied by drunken slurring he gave me one of the dog eared fivers. I popped the change I already had put aside into his hand. He opened the door after what seemed like an age, put both feet outside, stood up after what seemed another age and his trousers promptly fell down, giving me a fantastic view of his "interesting" underpants.

He tottered away from the car, pushed the door shut and pulled up his trousers. I filled my hire sheet in, using Mr H as the hirer's name, and kept an eye on him as he slowly crept to his house. Once he was inside, I pulled away and returned to the Black Bull and parked outside.

Mr H was behind the bar, with a few locals propping it up from their side as I walked in.

Me – Mr H. What was that guy's name?

Mr H – That was Daveyboy

Me – Oh. I couldn't understand a word he said

Bloke at bar (laughing) – No-one can

Me – I thought his name was Mister Azz Azz or something

Other bloke at bar (laughing) – That is his surname I think

Boss was delighted when he took over from me to do the evening shift. Davey turned into a very regular customer of ours who was one of the nicest guys to chat with when he was sober. When he'd had a few drinks though, all conversation went out the window.

Mr Gay – May 2008

On one of my very first Sunday shifts, Boss sent me up to Boyd's to take a Mr Day home around mid-afternoon. Boss described him as a senior gentleman and I thought nothing of it as I parked up outside. I could hear music through the walls and doorway as I ambled inside.

I opened the door to the bar area to find it was absolutely crammed to the rafters. It was as if everyone in Bellsbank was in there. The noise was unbearable and the big screen TV was showing the football. There were folks on pool tables, shouting, screaming and the heavy thud of very loud music. I had no idea what the guy looked like as I peered over the multitude of people I didn't know. I braced myself to walk in and scout round for a senior gentleman amongst the throng. I glanced down and saw a man sat on a wee stool just inside the door. "I wonder if he knows who Mr Day is," I thought. I stooped down to ask him. The noise in the bar was insane, so I got as close to this man as I could and shouted.

Me – You know a Mr Day?

Gentleman – Are you calling me gay?

Me – No sir! I'm asking if you know a Mr Day. I'm a taxi driver come for him

Gentleman – Let's go outside, it's too fuckin' noisy in here

We both stepped outside.

Gentleman – What's up, son?

Me (pointing to my cab) – I drive that taxi for Boss and I've come to collect a Mr Day and take him home. Do you know him?

Gentleman – Aye... It's me ya cunt. And don't fuckin' call me gay again. OK?

Me – Sir, I did not say you were gay. Sorry if it sounded like that

Gentleman – Nah, I'm fuckin' with ya kid. Come on let's get out of this place

Me (relieved) – Certainly, sir

I took the guy home and he was one of the nicest guys I ever had to deal with over the next few years. We occasionally chuckled over the "gay" incident and he would often say to his friends when I had a car full of them that I called him gay, and they'd be all shocked, then I'd pull a sad face, then Mr Day would confess I didn't call him gay... and so on. It was a pleasure to drive the guy and his mates home. One of them even started following West Bromwich Albion after he swiped my cap because he liked it. I let him keep it.

No Blow Job - June 2008

I got a call one Sunday afternoon to pick a guy up from Burnton and take him to Bellsbank. I didn't know who the guy was but he sounded OK on the phone so I went to pick him up expecting another incident-free hire. I pulled up outside his house and within a few seconds he appeared and was soon in the car. He was a young lad in his late teens. I can't recall his name because I only ever picked him up on this one occasion so he never became a regular, although this tale did stick in my memory for what will become obvious reasons.

Me – Afternoon, sir

Guy – All right, pal

Me – Bellsbank, sir?

Guy – Aye

He gave me the address and we were off. I was soon driving up the brae to Bellsbank.

Me – You OK there, bud? You look a bit... fed up to be honest

Guy – Oh well, it's the girlfriend

Me – Oh well the girlfriend, eh. Yes, I remember those. Ladies are very nice but they're tricky to handle I find

Guy – Aye. She won't suck my cock

I now thought, "Oh it's going to be one of those sorts of hires."

Me – Oh... right... hmm... yeah tricky one that, sir

Guy – Yeah, I mean I like having my cock sucked

Me – Well, who doesn't eh, sir?

Guy – Yeah

Me – Although I did hear of a guy from Birmingham who didn't like it

Guy – Really?

Me – Oh yes. I'm from Birmingham

Guy – Oh yes, I thought you sounded funny

Me – Yes, we all sound a bit like Ozzy Osbourne down there in Brum

Guy – Who?

Me – Doesn't matter. Er, so has your missus ever sucked your hampton?

Guy – Hampton?

Me – Aye... Hampton. Nob. Cock. Penis

Guy – Well yes, a few times but reluctantly. You ken?

Me – Reluctantly, eh. Have you performed the equivalent act on her? You know. Cunnilingus

Guy – Cunny, what now?

Me – You know, sir. Have you kissed her private area down below?

Guy – Oh well, she's not into that

Me – Hmm yes well... I take it that sir is clean in the hampton area. I did hear of a guy from Dudley who had a very dirty hampton and his missus wouldn't go near it

Guy – Yeah well... hmm... yeah good point, pal

Thankfully we had now arrived at his destination. He paid me and got out. I never saw him again. I often wonder how he got on with his missus. Did his final response of "good point, pal" mean anything? I'll never know.

The Whayr Road – July 2008

I stopped outside one of Dalmellington's sheltered accommodation complexes this one day to wait for one of my regulars, Richie. He was a single bloke in his late thirties who had just been visiting his grandmother. A big truck was squeezing its way through the village and stopped next to me, just as Richie emerged. The truck driver shouted over to him and I could hear every word of the brief exchange, although I pretended I didn't.

Truck driver – Excuse me, mate... where's the Ayr Road?

Richie – No idea pal... sorry

The truck driver pulled off without even asking me which I thought a bit odd. I was a taxi driver and may know where the Ayr Road is but there you go. Richie got in the taxi.

Me – Home, Richie?

Richie – Aye, John please

Me – What did that truck driver want?

Richie – The Ayr Road

Me – I trust that you put him right, eh

Richie – Er... no. I don't ken where the Ayr Road is

Me (glancing sideways) – You're joking, surely?

Richie – No, John. I haven't got a clue where the Ayr Road is

Me – Not a big traveller then?

Richie – I went to Falkirk once

Me – Yes... you told me about it... So you don't know where the Ayr Road is?

Richie – No

Me – Want to hazard a guess?

Richie – Er...

Me – Easy enough to work out, Richie. The clue is in the name of the road

Richie – The road that goes to Ayr past the filling station? I've been there on the 52 bus

Me – You'll make a taxi driver yet, mate... OK then, which is the Carsphairn Road?

Richie – Fuckin' hell, John, don't confuse me

Me – I'm sorry to say Richie that you've failed your taxi driver knowledge test

How we laughed, but a future story will illustrate that Richie did try to improve his geographical knowledge of the area. The people in the following two stories could maybe do the same.

Where's That? – August 2008

A young lass got in the taxi this one warm, sunny day. I can't remember her name and she was never a regular but I picked her up from the taxi office and took her to Bellsbank. As I drove up the brae from Dalmellington to Bellsbank she asked me both standard taxi driver questions.

Lass – What time you on 'til?

Me – Well that depends on his Bossness. Usually five pm on the day shift

Lass – Been busy?

Me – Not really although I've just had a hire down to Carsphairn which makes a nice change from all the local stuff

Lass – Carsphairn? Where's that?

Me – Er... the next village along the A713

Lass – I thought that was Patna?

Me – The other direction

Lass – The other direction?

Me – Yes. When you get to the bottom of the brae we've just driven up instead of turning left for Ayr... turn right

Lass – Ooh I've never been that way

Me – Oh

Where You Going Driver? – August 2008

The last in this quick trio of geographical stories involve a regular pair of middle-aged guys I took home from time to time. They were both Dalmellington born and bred, and sober. Funny how similar incidents occurred so close to each other too.

Depending on which direction my taxi was pointing and where folk wanted to go I'd either turn the car round or drive the way I was facing. Main Street was always pretty busy what with the buses and parked cars, but the High Street where the taxi office is situated was usually pretty quiet. So if they're going up to Bellsbank it was often quicker to drive up to the end of the High Street towards Carsphairn and Loch Doon then turn right at the end onto the A713, instead of battling past buses and trucks down the Main Street and turning left at the end. We operated a fixed fare system, so whichever way I went it cost the customer the same.

Eric and Sammy walked into the office and found me slumped in an armchair struggling with a particularly tricky level of Gem Drop on my phone. It's the game made for taxi drivers. Well it seemed like it the amount of time I spent playing.

Eric – Taxi up home, John please

Me – Aye, righto guys

I put my phone away, picked up my hire sheet, locked the office and we were soon in the car over the other side of the street. It was pointing away from the square towards Carsphairn. I started up and pulled away driving past an obvious turnaround point by the library next door.

Eric – Er... where you going, big 'un?

Me – You want Bellsbank?

Eric – Aye

Me – That's where we're going

Eric – Up here?

Me – Aye... up here

Eric – This road don't go to Bellsbank

Me – It does

Eric – It only goes to the loch

Me – I'll be turning right before then

Eric (to Sammy in the back) – Do you ken where this road goes?

Sammy – Aye... The loch

DIARY OF A TAXI DRIVER

Me – Aye, if you turn left at the end. I'll be turning right

We reached the junction with the A713. Left is towards the loch. Right is Bellsbank. I turned right.

Eric – Fuckin' hell! I ain't never been up here before

Sammy – I think I have years ago

Me – It's a wee bit further than going down Main Street but much less traffic

Eric – Well John, I'm amazed

Sammy – I've lived here all my life and always thought this road just went to the loch

Me – Just think guys, it took some ugly Brummie to show you where it actually went

How we laughed, but I found it incredible they didn't know where the road went.

The Kisser – September 2008

Debs was a very regular customer of ours. She often got a taxi for a run to the village shops then back home for various items once or twice a week, or she would ask me to pick an item up and drop it round next time I was passing. It was one of those hires I looked forward to. Debs was in her late fifties and we shared a similar sense of humour and I enjoyed our wee chats very much. I was particularly fond of her usage of industrial language in describing people we passed on our journeys, and how she referred to me as Dirty Brummie. Her husband Ewan was an average kind of guy in many ways, and a decent sort too, although I only ever had him in the taxi after he'd drunk rather large volumes of beer. This made him very, very friendly.

Boss shouted me to go and take Ewan home from Peggy's. I parked outside, walked in, tipped him the wink and stood by the door. When he emerged from the pub a minute or so later, I guided him into the front passenger seat, got in my seat, belted him in, asked him to stop kissing me, and we set off. It was a routine I'd done many, many times previously.

I asked him to stop kissing me all the way through the village and he took no notice whatsoever. Changing gear was the worst because my hand would momentarily be nearer to him and he'd pounce on it, trying to kiss it.

Ewan – Oh you're good to me and my missus John. You drive us wherever we want to go. Oh you're a good lad, mmmmm

Me – Ewan, I take lots of people where they want to go and they don't spend the entire journey trying to kiss me

Ewan – Well they don't realise what a nice chap you are, mmmmm

Me (trying not to laugh) – We're nearly at your place now so stop trying to kiss me, please

I pulled up outside his house and went round to his side, opened his door and helped him out fending off some kisses. I took his arm and wedged my right forearm under his left armpit to steady us for the few steps down to his garden path. He seemed a wee bit more under the influence today I thought as we went through the open gate. He seemed to weigh more, or I was holding him up more than usual. Debs watched us through her lounge window.

Then we fell down the steps and his head hit my stomach just as I landed on my back on the grass. I saw stars and felt the breath disappear from my lungs. I could barely breathe. I could hear shouting and screaming. Ewan lay motionless until Debs, who had dashed out, moved him with her foot.

I looked around and a neighbour came to help me. Debs continued to make abrupt comments to her husband while she poked him with something.

Neighbour – You OK, John?

Me – I think so. What happened?

Neighbour – Ewan fell on you

Me – Oh! Is he OK?

Debs – Fuck him. As long as you're OK that's all I'm bothered about

Me – I'll be OK if I just sit here a minute or so

Ewan stirred and looked over to me.

Ewan – You OK, big 'un?

Me – Aye, I'm OK, Ewan

Debs – No thanks to you

Ewan – I'm sorry, John

Me – No harm done, Ewan

Ewan – Let me kiss it better, mmmmm

I suddenly felt a lot better and stood up with the neighbour helping me.

Debs – Did he pay you, John?

Me – No not yet, Debs

Debs – Here

And she gave me much more than the fare. Ewan blew a kiss at me and I limped back to the taxi, waved, and drove off. My stomach ached for ages.

Bang On Time – October 2008

Over the years I'd had various events occur in and around the taxi. Funnily enough it was only ever just one instance of each type of event. One actual attempt at punching me, one instance of a passenger vomiting, although she aimed it all out the door brilliantly, once instance of me completely forgetting a hire because I didn't write it on the booking sheet, and so on. I also prided myself on being on time every time. Someone would book a taxi for 1 pm and I'd get to the pick up at... ooh say twelve fifty-nine pm. That kind of thing.

I decided to see just how accurate I could be. I set the clock in the car to internet time. I also decided that the hire would start at the exact second my customer got in and shut the door, not when I pulled up outside or they came out their house.

The days and weeks went by and I was my usual one or two minutes early for the vast majority of hires, and maybe a few minutes late for the odd hire here and there. I'd look at the clock as they got in and hoped the time would flick to the exact hire time as the door shut, but it never did.

Then Emma phoned up one day about twelve thirty pm. She was a nice lass in her twenties who I knew well as she used Boss's taxis a lot.

Me – Hello, T&C Taxis

Emma – Oh is that you, John? I need a taxi at one o'clock down to the square and back up to home, please

I knew without looking at the booking sheet I could do Emma's hire easily.

Me – OK no probs. I'll get you at 1 pm. You at home, I take it?

Emma – Aye

Me – Catch you in thirty minutes then

Emma – Cheers, John

I knew where she lived, so there was no need to clutter up the conversation with questions like "What's the pick-up address, madam?" and it meant I could spend more precious time on Gem Drop, the taxi driver's best friend.

At an appropriate time to get to Emma's for one pm, I drove up to her place at the very end of Bellsbank and I pulled up outside her house at twelve fifty-nine. Within a few seconds she was out of her front door and in the taxi. The clock on the dashboard changed to one pm at the exact same second that she shut the car door. I pointed at the clock.

Me – I'm great. I'm probably the best taxi driver in Britain. I deserve a timekeeping gold medal...

Emma (butting in) – What's the time, John?

Me – Er... One o'clock Emma. Exactly when you wanted me. I'm great, aren't I?

Emma – Fuck!

Me – Er... what's up?

Emma – The fuckin' chemist shuts at one

Me – Does it?

Emma – I think so

Me – I honestly don't know

I didn't know.

Emma – Oh fuck, John

Me – Well, I've got time for a quick one, I suppose

Emma (missing my rubbish joke) – Can you come and get me at two? I think they reopen then

Me – You sure, Emma?

Emma – Aye... come and get me at two please, John

I quickly scanned my booking sheet and she was in luck.

Me – OK, I'll get you at two

Emma – Great... cheers, John

I didn't charge her for that cancelled hire because I had a hire in Bellsbank in fifteen minutes anyway. I just paid a visit to the shop, stocked up on chewing gum and played Gem Drop until my next hire which I was two minutes early for. At two o'clock I was about one minute early for Emma. The only hire I ever specifically remember being absolutely bang on time for was over as soon as it had started.

Road Numbers - November 2008

Ever since the Ayr Road Question Incident I must admit I did poke fun at Richie from time to time. He ribbed me back and it was all jolly good banter we both enjoyed. One day he called for a cab and within a few minutes I'd picked both him and his mother up from their house in Bellsbank and headed down the brae to Dalmellington.

A few weeks before, Richie had phoned for a taxi and I dutifully pulled up outside his house where I found him carrying some stepladders. I got out of the taxi and he asked if he could put the ladders in the boot. I pulled a face of astonishment and asked why he didn't mention the ladders on the phone. I could have brought a bigger vehicle. I don't think he understood. I folded the back seats down, took out the parcel shelf and the ladders thankfully fitted in snugly with a firm shove. Richie noted that the ladders fitted in the car so couldn't see a problem. Yes... Quite.

Back to the current hire.

Richie – I've been doing some thinking, John

Me – Thinking of moving a canoe are you? Or a piano maybe?

Richie – Oh the stepladders again... John they fitted in the boot, man. You worry too much

Me – Yes, I worry we may not get a four poster bed in here

Richie – Listen, I've been doing some thinking

Mother (laughing) – Och, you'll get a headache, son

Richie – Ha, ha, very funny... Yeah so these roads... they have numbers as well as names I noticed... on the road signs

Mother – Pity you don't notice all that mess in your room that needs tidying up, you lazy pig

Richie – Mother... I'm asking John a question

Me – Go on, mate

I turned left onto the A713

Richie – What's this one we're on now? The number I mean

Me – This road is the A713.... and soon we'll be turning right onto the B741 which is the Main Street

Richie – Why have they all got different numbers?

Me (stunned) – Er... er... er... er... Good question, Richie

Richie (to his mum) – See... good question

Me – It's hard to explain unless you actually drive... which you don't

Richie – Aha he doesn't ken, mum! Bloody hell John I thought you would have known that. Wait until I tell Boss. Whoo he'll laugh

We arrived at their destination and they got out leaving me to ponder his question. Obviously I knew why, but it was hard to explain in the fifty yards left on the journey. I didn't ponder for long and drifted back to normality. Boss did tell me a few days later that Richie mentioned I didn't know why roads have different numbers. Boss told him the A1 was the first road to be built, the A2 was the second and so on. Richie explained this to me the next time I saw him and I said that Boss did know a lot about roads and stuff so he was probably right.

Parcel Delivery Man

As well as taxi driving, I did a bit of parcel delivery work now and then. We covered some parcel runs in nearby towns and villages for friends of Boss when they were on holiday or sick. We actually got a parcel round of our own at one point. That ended after a few years when the driver who dropped parcels off at our taxi office in the mornings, tried to palm Boss and myself off with an item for somewhere well out of our area. We knew exactly what areas we delivered to, the Cumnocks, but this guy was very insistent we have a roll of carpet for somewhere down near Stranraer. It got a bit heated between him and us, and "industrial language" and "ungentlemanly conduct" went on. Suffice it to say we lost the parcel contract.

The parcels were all Next, Readers Digest, Freeman's etc... catalogue stuff... Over the years I delivered to every town and village in a twenty mile radius and got to know the area very well. It made a change from driving the taxi, although I did the deliveries in the taxi as there usually weren't many to get through in a day. And although according to Richie in the previous story, I didn't know why roads had different numbers, I did know that houses having numbers, or names, were the key to identifying them.

Invisible Farm

Poor or missing house numbers and signs were a sore topic for me and probably other delivery people. It was especially so if they were new to an area, or was one of those areas which wasn't planned out very well, or through various stages of growth, had left a seemingly random house numbering system. The number of times I couldn't see a house number on a property was astonishing. There simply wasn't a number or name anywhere. Or there were houses that had a black number on a black background, or white on white. Or someone painted the door and went straight over the number.

Now usually, number 1 is on the left side of a road as you come off a main street and move away from the centre of a conurbation, and number 2 is opposite, but not always. The time I wasted looking for a house added up to hours. I swear that some streets are numbered by someone just drawing balls out of a bag like the FA Cup draw.

Farms were a pain sometimes. Most had a big sign at the end of the usually very long driveway, but I was looking for a particular farm one day and getting nowhere. All the farms on this road seemed to have signs at the road end and I'd delivered to many of them over the years. I asked a guy walking his dog and he guided me to where it was and told me there's no sign for it. I found the drive which looked like a field entrance really, drove down the potholed mud track, and knocked at the door of the house that eventually appeared behind a wall of trees. Invisible from the main road. A lady answered, and I told her I had a hard job finding her place because there was no sign. She laughed. I expressed my woe again and laid on a bit of a story about the thirty minutes I had wasted all for the want of a sign. She laughed again and said, "Hmm... I ken."

No House Sign

Before I set out on my round, I had a look through the paperwork or gadget to see if there were any unusual addresses or remote farms I wasn't sure of. This one day I had a parcel for a place called The Nest. I knew which road it was on, a long road, but not which house.

Me – Boss, I've got one here for The Nest

Boss – Aye, that's on Suchandsuch Road

Me – Aye, I know it

Boss – There are two houses set apart from the rest of the street. They're much older than the rest by a wee brig over a burn

Me – I think I know the ones you mean

Boss – Well I'm not sure which house is which out of the two, but one is The Nest and the other is The Cottage

Me – Oh well that's easy enough to work out when I get there

I stopped at these two houses first on my way in at about 8 am as they're near the Dalmellington side of this particular town. No signs or anyone at home at either house, and there was no-one else around I could ask. I did the rest of my round and called in again a wee while later around mid-afternoon on my way back to base.

I went to the house on the left and a man answered the door.

Me – Is this The Nest?

Man (annoyed) – No, it's next door. This is The Cottage

Me – Sorry sir, but I couldn't see a house sign

He firmly shut the door and I tried the other house. A lady answered my knocking.

Me – Is this The Nest?

I know it may seem a redundant question, since I had eliminated next door from being The Nest, but I liked to make my point.

Lady – Yes it is. Ooh one of my parcels has arrived

I gave her the parcel and she signed the gadget.

Me – I came here earlier but I couldn't establish which house was which out the two here. This house and The Cottage next door. No house signs you see

Lady – Didn't the man next door tell you it was here?

Me – He wasn't in either. Do you rely on him being in to direct people here? I think a sign might be a more efficient way

Lady – Oh... the other parcel guy puts my stuff in the shed out the back if I'm out

Me – Yes, but he knows which house is which. I'm new on this round

Lady – Oh...

Me – A sign would have helped

Lady – ... (silence)

Just then, and I am not putting this in here for dramatic effect, (it actually happened) another delivery guy arrived, parked up and shouted up from the road.

Delivery Guy – Which is The Nest out of these two houses?

Me – I'm off, madam. Point made I think

I could tell by the expression on her face that she just didn't see the problem. A friend of mine delivered parcels for a while and he said he had trouble finding a house one day that he eventually discovered in a small forest down a long unmarked driveway. He informed the householder of the trouble he'd had finding the place, to which he received the reply, "well the house has been here three hundred years and other people find it."

In short, can I offer this advice to people, and if only a few houses get better signage I'll feel like I've achieved something. Make sure your house has a number or name on it that can be seen and read from the road. It might not be a guy delivering a parcel next time.

The Wife

I knocked on the door of one particular house, a man answered, and it went something like this

Me – Parcel for Mrs Bloggs

Man – Well I'm not Mrs Bloggs, am I?

Me – Well no sir, but perhaps you know a Mrs Bloggs here?

Man – Aye, the wife probably

Me (giving an arm pump) – Yeah, we found her!

Sarcastic I know, but what are they going to do? I couldn't get away with cheek like this in the taxi, so I dished it out on the parcel runs.

Bingo Street

I was looking for a number 8A in one particular street. There was a group of four houses with no numbers on at all, with the houses around them seemingly numbered by a bingo caller, so I couldn't fathom out which house may have been 8A. I saw a curtain twitch so I walked up the path. I knocked on the door and a man answered.

Me – Is this 8A?

Man (sighing) – No, this is 8. 8A is next door

Me – Sorry, but there's no numbers on a few houses around here

Man – Yes, I get this a lot

Me – Get what, sir?

Man – People knocking on my door when they want 8A or 9 or 8B or 7 and all sorts. Gets on my nerves it does

Me – Yes, I can see that would get annoying. Hey! I've got an idea

Man – What's that?

Me – Go down the D-I-Y shop and buy a number and stick it on your door. Or even draw one on in felt tip pen.

Man – Nah, why should I?

Me – Yeah, good point. Much easier to keep answering the door I guess. Bye, sir

It seemed an obvious solution to me but there you go.

Postcode

I got to number 52 in this one street. No-one was in, the parcel was too big for the letterbox and the dog in the back garden put me off trying the shed or greenhouse. I stepped next door to number 50 where I saw a middle-aged lady having a wee nosey. I knocked and she came to the door.

Me – I've got a parcel for Mr Neverin at 52 but he's out. Would you take it?

Lady – Sure

The lady kindly took the parcel and placed it on the side table in her hallway out of my view. I now need to enter some details into the barcode scanner gadget I've got. I could see the lady's mother hovering in the background. The lady told me her name so I punched that in. I entered the address (which I could work out for myself) and first half of her postcode. The entire town I was delivering to begins with the same postcode area so I just needed the last two letters of the lady's postcode.

Me – Last two letters of your postcode please, madam?

Lady – AB

I entered it into the scanner, the lady signed it and we were done.

Me – Thank you, madam

Lady – Not at all. Mr Neverin is a nice man and it's a pleasure to help

By now the lady's mother had shuffled closer.

Me – Thank you ladies, I'll be off now

Mother – Er, Mr Parcelman

Me (turning) – Yes, madam

Mother – Don't you know all your postcodes then?

Me – Sorry, madam?

Mother – Shouldn't you know all the postcodes where you deliver to?

Lady (embarrassed) – Oh mother!

Me – Yes, you're quite right. I'll get onto it right away

Mother – I should think so too

Lady (quietly to me) – Sorry

Me (quietly back) – No problem. Take care

Even to this day I can remember the postcode of that lady's house, but I sadly didn't manage to learn the postcode of every house in the town.

What Number Is This?

I got to number 55 in this particularly upmarket street in the nice part of town and no-one was in, so I tried number 57 next door. A smartly dressed lady in her fifties answered.

Me – Sorry to bother you madam but I'm delivering this parcel to number 55 and...

Her (butting in) – What number did you say?

Me – 55, madam

She pointed at the big shiny number 57 on her front door.

Her (adopting sarcastic tone) – And what number is this?

Me – 57, madam

Her (talking to me like I was an eight-year-old) – And what number are you delivering to?

Me – 55, madam

Her (folding her arms like she'd won) – So why are you knocking on my door?

Me – Because number 55 are out and I thought that you may be good enough to take their parcel. If it's a problem I'll try elsewhere or just take the parcel back to the office

Her (realising her mistake) – Oh yes... er... quite... oh sure, yes... er... of course I'll take the... er... parcel

Don't assume so much, madam.

Ask The Obvious

This story could happen to anyone at any time, but it happened to me when I was on one of my parcel rounds in the taxi.

I was just about to pull in the lay-by at a shop in New

Cumnock I frequented so I could grab a quick bite to eat. I was about half way through my parcel round this one rainy day and I needed a break. As I pulled in, the back left tyre went down in seconds. Damn! I knew without looking it was a puncture. And it was throwing it down with rain. I braced myself for a speedy wheel change, but decided to grab a coffee and sausage roll from the shop first and wait for the rain to ease off. On my quick sprint into the shop, I glared at the flat tyre and waved my fist at it.

I sat back in the car, ate and drank for about twenty minutes and the rain never eased off. It got heavier. I had changed a few wheels in my time, so I wasn't worried, just fed up that it was so wet. Two men were huddled under the shop canopy now so I'd have an audience too.

Deciding to just get on with it, I got out, whipped the boot open, got the spare out, leant it against the flat tyre and quickly took cover for a minute under the canopy to gather my thoughts.

Man 1 – Not nice having a puncture in this weather, laddie

Me – I know. I'll have it done soon enough though

Man 2 – The rain ain't going to ease off for you either, pal

Me – No it isn't... Right, here I go lads

I got the jack out the boot, lifted the car a wee bit, then started taking the wheel nuts off... then another man appeared out the shop and stood with the others.

Bloke – What you doing, pal?

Me – What? What am I doing?

The other two guys looked on and I could see them shaking their heads.

Bloke – Aye... what you doing?

Man 1 – What the fuck do you think he's doing?

Man 2 – Aye. Damn stupid question really pal

Me – I'm wallpapering my spare room. What does it look like I'm doing?

Bloke – Only asking

Me (still undoing nuts) – Why ask? What's the bloody point?

Bloke – Puncture, is it?

Me – WHAT? Of course it's a fuckin' puncture! I wouldn't be changing the wheel in this bleedin rain for the fun of it, would I? Would I, eh?

Man 1 – What a fuckin' idiot

Bloke – Won't bother asking again

Me (sarcasm at maximum) – Oh no. Please ask again

Man 2 – Fuck's sake eh. What a clown!

Make conversation with people by all means, but think about what you're saying for goodness sake.

We Don't Deliver Parcels Any More

I was stood outside the taxi office late one weekday afternoon doing nothing other than watching sleepy Dalmellington go about its business and thinking of maybe having another attempt at a tricky level of Gem Drop, when a senior lady appeared into view. She was smartly dressed with an air of decorum and grace about her. I'd seen her floating about the village but never had her as a passenger in the taxi so therefore had no idea who she was.

She walked straight past me to the office door but it was locked. I never left it open, even if I was just outside in case I got called away and forgot to lock it.

Me – Yes, madam ... where to?

Lady – I want to return this parcel to Boss

Me – Are you from Dalmellington, madam?

Lady – Och, yes I am

Me – Let me see

I took a wee look at the parcel and it was a catalogue jobby like we used to do, but it was addressed to somewhere in Stranraer which is at least fifty miles down the A77. Pete, a guy from Patna, delivered Dalmellington and surrounding areas and I covered his round now and then when he was off on holidays or poorly. This parcel was way off Pete's round but the lady said she was from the village. Delivered in error, I assumed.

We lost the contract to deliver Cumnock and New Cumnock months back so we didn't deliver anything at all now, except for the wee arrangement with Pete. It was an arrangement he had with Boss as they were both mates from years gone by. Either way we could only have taken returns from our round which we didn't have any more, not Pete's round.

Me – This is for an address in Stranraer

Lady – I know... It's not for me... I live just up the road

Me – You get deliveries regularly? Or is this a one-off?

Lady – Och yes, I'm always buying wee things for the grandchildren and so on

Me – Hmm... And now somehow you've ended up with a parcel which should be fifty miles away... Most odd... Oh well Boss isn't here and we don't do parcels any more. Your best option would be to either give it to Pete next time you see him, phone the catalogue company or take it to the Post Office. They handle returns I think. I'm not sure to be honest how to return items because I only delivered them

The last time I'd covered Pete's round was months previously, and I couldn't fathom out how this lady had a parcel with a Stranraer address on it. How did it get delivered to her? Even if I had covered Pete's round in the past few weeks, I don't think I'd have delivered a parcel for Stranraer to a house round here. The address on it didn't exist in the village.

Lady – Is this Boss's taxi place?

Me – Yes

Lady – Is he here?

Me – No, just me

Lady – Well, normally he's here

Me – He's out in Ayr getting car parts

This was my usual response when folk asked where Boss was.

Lady – Who are you?

Me – John. I drive taxis for Boss

Lady – Oh... and he's not here?

Me – Sadly not, or else I'd direct you to him... and we don't do parcels any more so I don't think he'll want this return. Actually I'll rephrase that. We couldn't take that return because we don't deliver parcels any more, and haven't delivered them for months

The lady looked around and toyed with the parcel in her hand.

Lady – Well, who delivered it then?

Me – I reckon it would be Pete. So I think you should maybe hand it back to him next time you see him

Lady – Pete?

Me – Yes... he delivers the Doon Valley area

Lady (like she'd never heard of the area she lived in) – Doon Valley?

Me – Yes... Dalmellington, Bellsbank, Patna, Dalrymple and Corton in Alloway

Lady – Don't know him

Me – Maybe it's a new guy then... I really don't know

Lady – It's a man in a van normally

Me – Well that could be anyone really

Lady – Boss has got a van

Me – Yes he has... but we don't deliver parcels any more

Lady – I'm sure Boss has delivered parcels to me in the past

Me – Maybe he did in the past but since last November we don't do parcels any more

Lady – Yes you do... Boss delivers them

I knew for a fact that Boss hadn't covered Pete's round lately either. I think the last time Boss delivered parcels in the village would be at least twelve months previously. I was also not going to mention the fact that we occasionally covered Pete's deliveries in the village. That would confuse an already messy situation.

Me – We used to deliver Cumnock and New Cumnock anyway not this area

Lady – Not here?

Me – No... Pete delivers round here

Lady – Where's this Pete?

Me – Pete lives in Patna

Lady (incredulous) – Patna!

Me – Yes, Patna. He drives a grey VW van I think. Might be a

Toyota. Not sure...

Lady – I want to give this parcel to Boss

Me (wishing the lady would understand what I'm saying) – He's driving and will not answer his phone. I'll try and get Pete's number

I looked in the taxi phone. Boss had people's names listed in the most ridiculous fashion known to man. He'd have Mr Smith listed under "M" for Mister and so on. I couldn't find Pete under "P" and I didn't know his surname either so my search was fruitless.

Me – Sorry, but I can't find Pete's number in the phone. Boss will have it somewhere I imagine. Probably in his personal phone rather than the taxi phone

Lady – Is Boss not in?

I think I nearly passed out at this point

Me (opting for the "explain it to death" method) – No, Boss is not in. He's driven to Ayr... fifteen miles away... to get some spares for an 02 plate Vauxhall Vectra saloon. I suggest you phone the taxi number later after six pm when Boss is on duty. I won't be around then so Boss will take your call. Here's a card with the taxi number on it. After six o'clock, OK?

Lady (finally getting it) – Er, OK then

Funny thing is I simply cannot remember if Boss spoke to her later and I never discovered how she ended up with a parcel that should be fifty miles down the road. I wondered if it was something to do with the guy who tried to palm a carpet off on Boss and me that one time too. I also don't think I'd ever met anyone sober who was so slow or reluctant to understand a situation. I also don't think I'd ever repeated a phrase (in this instance "we don't do parcels any more") so many times in such a short period of time.

Knickers - March 2009

Back in the taxi once again and it was a nice average Friday morning when I did the regular trip to pick up Alison and take her down to the Black Bull for a regular session she enjoyed there with friends. I liked Alison and she always gave me a cigarette when I dropped her off at the pub. Throughout the day I did all my usual runs, then around five pm Boss shouted me over the radio to go to the Black Bull, collect Alison and take her home.

I never picked her up from the Bull normally. Either Boss collected her, or her daughter would pick her up. I usually finished around five o'clock but Boss had yet more paperwork to attend to so I worked on a bit longer. I drove down from Bellsbank, pulled up outside the Bull, opened the pub door and Alison was stood just a yard or so inside the doorway swaying gently.

Me – Oh hello, Alison. Taxi for you

Alison (heavily slurred) – OK, John

I let the pub door gently swing to and waited by the car so I could open the car door for her. I waited... and I waited... and I waited. I thought I'd better go check what was going on. I opened the pub door...and she hadn't moved an inch.

Me – You OK, Alison?

Alison – Aye, John

Me (offering an arm) – Take my arm

She did so and tottered one leg in front of the other as we inched towards the door. Then her fags and keys fell out of her handbag onto the floor.

Me – I'll get those

Alison – Thanks John, you're good

I bent down to retrieve them and Alison's trousers fell down, promptly followed by her knickers! They slid down inches from my face. One word raced through my head. "No!"

Alison – Ooh John, I'm in a bit of a mess. My trousers have fallen down

Me – Er, um, er, um

Alison – Help me, John

I'm normally capable of making quick decisions, but I simply had no idea what to do. Her top was long and nearly reached her knees so considering the situation she was "decent". I peeked into the pub to see if there was anyone who fancied helping out, but they were all laughing. I spied a wee chair close at hand, took a few steps, grabbed it and placed it directly behind Alison. She dropped into it.

Me – Hang on, Alison. I got to see Boss for a second

In a few large bounds I reached the sanctuary of the taxi office. Actually the taxi office was a bit of a mess most of the time. Cross a teenager's bedroom with some Vauxhall Vectra spares and a sea of untidy paperwork and you're nearly there.

Me – No way, Boss. No way

Boss – What's wrong?

Me – Alison is in the Bull with her trousers and knickers round her ankles. I don't know what to do

Boss – Not again! That woman needs to get some elastic in her trousers. She did this with me a few weeks ago outside the Spar.

Me – What do we do?

Boss –Well, you're not taking her anywhere that's for sure. We can't get involved in that nonsense. Anyone in the pub?

Me – Aye, they're all laughing

Boss – For fuck's sake! I'll phone her daughter up. Go and tell Alison that we can't take her

So I trotted back over the road and while I looked at the pub carpet, I explained to Alison that I couldn't take her home. We'd phone her daughter. I trotted back over to the taxi office where Boss was on the phone explaining the situation to Alison's daughter. I went back outside and lit a cigarette. Alison's daughter arrived in her car after a few minutes, gave me a look that said "Sorry" and went in the Bull. She reappeared a few minutes later with Alison and took her home. I still don't know what I'd do in a similar situation. I try to imagine what would have happened, or what it would look like, if I'd tried to help and she'd fallen over or something. Thankfully, Alison didn't get into such a state in future.

Cakes – April 2009

Boss was controlling the office this one day while he attended to reams of tiresome paperwork and I went about a pleasant day's taxi driving. The sun was out and everything was going routinely when he shouted me over the radio.

Boss – TC6, what's your position?

Me – Just finished off a hire in Bellsbank. Returning to the office now

Boss – There's a lady in the office who requires your services TC6

Me – Roger, Control. Five minutes

Boss (laughing) – Not good enough TC6

Me (pretend seriousness) – I'm doing my very best Boss

Boss (laughing) – Aye well TC6 your best is merely adequate

Me – I beg to differ, Control. I'm the best Brummie taxi driver this village has ever seen

Boss – Just get back here

Whoever was waiting in the office could hear this exchange, and I knew that Boss liked to banter when certain folk could overhear. Boss and myself had a very good working relationship. He had off days like we all do, but I liked the guy and I think he liked me. We're still friends now and often chat on the phone. I drove back to the office and pulled up outside.

Me (radio) – TC6 outside

Boss – Come in TC6. The lady has a lot of messages

I got out the car and went in the office and it was June, one of my regular senior ladies.

June – Oh hello John, I need a run up to home please

Me – Certainly

June followed me out the office as I carried all of her messages barring two wee bags. We placed it all in the boot, and were soon on our way.

Me – Lovely spring day, June

June – Oh yes John. You and Boss have a good laugh on the radio I heard. You two make me laugh

Me – Aye June, we try and have a laugh because this job can be hard at times. One minute I'm taking a nice lady like yourself home. The next minute... who knows? Some drunken oaf or verbal abuse maybe.

We carried on chatting, and soon arrived at her house. Again I took the bulkiest bags and followed behind June who carried the two wee bags. We walked up her slabbed pathway which bent sharply to the left and continued our wee chat. She looked behind to say something and stumbled, falling like a felled tree. Luckily her head missed the path as it bent left just at the right moment, so her face landed in soft border soil she hadn't yet planted.

Quick as a flash I placed my bags down and gently helped her. She cried and I wiped the loose soil from her face. Once she'd regained a bit of composure I helped her up, found her key, opened the door and escorted her into the kitchen and sat her down. I put the kettle on, then nipped outside to retrieve the shopping. I returned and found a kitchen towel to clean up her face. I couldn't see any cuts or abrasions.

Me – June are you OK? You feel any pain?

June (sobbing) – Och no John, I just feel such a fool

Me – June you're far from a fool. A mate of mine tripped over a sausage once... No cuts or blood June. I'll phone Boss and tell him I'm staying here a while to look after you OK

My true story cheered her up and I made her a cup of tea. I then phoned Boss who then phoned June's daughter. I waited with June to make sure she was OK until her daughter arrived about ten minutes later, then returned to the office and quickly got back to the job.

The next day Boss and myself were stood outside the office talking pish, when June ambled down the street carrying a large grocery bag. She approached us with a big smile on her face.

June – These are for you

She handed me the bag and it was full of wee cakes.

June – I made them for you last night, John. You were so good to me when I fell over

I thanked her and was relieved she was OK. Her face did look a bit sore but I think the soil being so soft acted like a cushion.

I was so glad she didn't stumble a few feet earlier and hit the slabs instead. The cakes were fantastic and I even let Boss have one or two.

Father and Son – April 2009

Saturdays tended to have no real pattern except that if it was raining or cold I was busier than if it was dry and sunny. This one day was dry with just the odd wee shower so I was pretty quiet. The quietness was added to by the horse racing at Ayr which a number of locals travelled to for a fun day out. Up until 1 pm all was quiet and normal. I was sat in the office after clearing some junk off one of the broken armchairs, drinking coffee that had been microwaved a few times that morning and played Gem Drop on my phone. Natalie, the part-time weekend office girl, alternated between texting her mates and catching up on Boss's paperwork. A thump against the door broke the silence.

Natalie – John, there's some really drunken looking bloke at the door

Me (having a wee peek) – Oh, that's Rocky. He probably wants a taxi just up to home

Rocky stumbled in the office.

Me – You wanting home, Rocky?

Rocky – New fuckin' Cumnock... Me and the lad. He's in the

fuckin' Railway. Come on!

Me – New Cumnock, eh... I'll have a look at my bookings

Rocky swayed gently in the waiting room while I checked the booking sheet. My next hire wasn't until 2 pm.

Me – You're in luck Rocky. Let's go

Rocky – Good. Let's get Alex from the Railway. I won five hundred quid on the horses today in the bookies. We're gonna get blootered in New fuckin' Cumnock

Me – Cool. Natalie, I'll be back before 2 o'clock. I'll radio you when I'm back in the village

Natalie – OK, John

We got in the cab and in seconds we arrived at The Railway just yards away. I went in to get Alex. He was about twenty and his dad was in his mid-forties. He swayed gently in front of a fruit machine.

Me – Alex

Alex (kicking the machine) – Fuckin' machine!

Me – Alex! Your dad is off to New Cumnock and you're coming too apparently

Alex – What?! Cumnock?

Me – No. New Cumnock. Come on Alex. He's in my taxi now

Alex – OK, pal.

Alex swilled his remaining beer down his neck and staggered violently out of the Railway. I got in the taxi. Rocky was in the front seat. Alex shouted obscenities at his father through the window. His dad replied with abuse and threats of violence. Alex eventually got in and I pulled away wishing the next twenty minutes would just vanish to be honest.

Rocky – We're gonna show New Cumnock how Dalmellington boys handle their drink

Alex – Aye... and I'm gonna shag some Cumnock lassies

Me – Alex, we're going to New Cumnock... not Cumnock

Alex – Aye, New fuckin' Cumnock then

The road to New Cumnock from the village is tight and swooping and I knew it well. I listened to father and son engage in a conversation about boozing, shagging ladies and gambling. I also wondered how much more booze they could drink.

Rocky – How much is this fuckin' taxi, big 'un?

Me – £13.60p, Rocky

Rocky – Will you come and get us later?

Me – When?

Rocky – 1 am... just get us, OK

Me – Can't be done. Boss has got a hire then, I know that. A regular we get every week

Rocky – OK then whenever. Just come and get us

Me – I'll get a time with the office. Hang on

I radioed Natalie before I lost the signal and we agreed that twelve fifteen am was fine.

Me – Twelve fifteen then lads, OK?

Rocky – Aye, OK, but you'd better fuckin' be there

Me – I won't but Boss will get you, OK?

Rocky – Aye, OK

Me – And you'll have to pay me up front so that will be £27.20p, OK?

Rocky handed me £30.00

Rocky – Enough?

Me – Aye plenty, Rocky. Boss will get you later

Rocky – Keep the change, big 'un

Me – Cheers, Rocky

More nonsense and swearing at each other followed as we drove along the road to New Cumnock. Eventually we got there and I could feel that relief from the earache was near at hand.

Me – Where to then lads?

Rocky – The Brig Inn

I had delivered parcels in New Cumnock and I liked to think I knew it pretty well. There wasn't a Brig Inn I knew of. There was Glens Bar, The Clutch Bar, a working men's club and a hotel that was closed.

Me – Never heard of it

Rocky – It's down here for fuck's sake

Rocky gestured violently at a row of houses and shops.

Me – There's no pub there Rocky. All I see is a butcher's shop. The working men's is just up the road

Rocky – Fuckin' take us there then

I pulled up in the working men's club car park.

Me – Phone Boss later about ten... eleven o'clock just to make sure he's coming for you but I'll check myself that Nat has written it on the sheet OK

Rocky – We ain't got a phone

Me – Fu.... OK Boss will get you at fifteen after midnight... from here. I'll make sure, OK guys?

Rocky – You fuckin' better big 'un

Me – No worries Rocky

They staggered out the taxi and pushed and shoved each other all the way to the door of the working men's club. I drove off and stopped at a wee shop just down the road (where I had the puncture and stupid questions) to get a quick bite to eat before I headed back to pick up my two pm hire. I opted for a pastie and coffee and returned to an exciting level of Gem Drop once I was back in the taxi.

After a few minutes I realised I'd messed up the timings. I need to get Boss to pick them up at midnight at the very latest so he could get back to Patna, not Dalmellington, for the regular hire. I started the car and readied myself for the short drive back to the club, and lo and behold, both Rocky and Alex were staggering down the road towards me. I got out the car and shouted over to them.

Me – Rocky! Boss will have to get you at midnight at the very latest, OK?

Rocky – Aye OK, big 'un. The Brig Inn is down there by the butchers. We'll be there, OK?

Me – Aye, OK. Midnight then

They staggered off. I got back in my cab and scoffed my pastie while thinking that Boss would hopefully know where the apparently invisible Brig Inn was. Maybe I should ask in the butcher's. I drove off and timed it just right as I saw Alex and Rocky enter a plain looking front door by the butcher's shop. The Brig Inn was scrawled on a cardboard sign above the door. At least I knew where it was now, and I could act all knowledgeable with Boss when I saw him later and explain where it was if he didn't know already. Highly unlikely Boss wouldn't know, but the thought of knowing something he didn't made me smile a wee bit.

Anyway I drove back to Dalmellington and got back nicely in time to get my two o'clock hire from the Co-op. The day progressed fairly normally over the next hour or so, then I spotted Alex running through the village in a violently drunken manner which I thought was a bit odd. I then went for a hire in Ayr to collect a regular from the races so I was out the village for the next hour. I dropped them off and radioed back to base.

Me – TC6 clear in Park Crescent

Natalie – TC6, can you come back to the office please?

Me – Roger

I pulled up right outside the office two minutes later.

Me (over the radio) – TC6 outside

Usually folk came to the office and waited for a cab. I sat outside and waited for them to emerge.

Natalie (radio) – You'll have to come in, John

Me – OK

I thought that maybe it was someone with bulky heavy messages. I was wrong. It was Rocky… and he was asleep on the least cluttered armchair.

Natalie – He's been here a while now since you've been out doing that hire from Ayr

Me – Where does he want to go?

Natalie – Bellsbank

Me – Easy enough

Natalie – Yes, but some guy called Alex in the Black Bull wants a taxi now as well. The barmaid phoned about ten minutes ago

Me – Probably Rocky's lad, Alex

Natalie – Oh... well take them both then I guess

Me (nudging the chair) – Rocky!

Rocky woke up.

Me – Bellsbank then, mate? You going home?

Rocky – Am I fuck. I'm going to Birdie's

I had no idea who or what "Birdie's" was, but after a couple of years in the job I reckoned I could work it out somehow.

Me – Er... OK, is your lad coming with us?

Rocky – That cunt? Aye. Where the fuck is he?

Me – Over the road I think. Let's go get him

Rocky got on his feet and we stepped outside. Dawn the barmaid over the road was having a cigarette. She saw us and gave me a wee nod. She shouted back into the pub.

Dawn – Alex! Your dad's getting a taxi with John up the road

Alex emerged seconds later staggering violently and almost falling over numerous times.

Alex – What's that stupid cunt doing now?

Rocky – Shut the fuck up, you silly wee cunt! Get in this fuckin' taxi!

Alex – Ah bollocks, you silly old cunt

Alex moved back towards the pub. Dawn intercepted him and guided him across the pavement towards the taxi. Rocky and Alex met in the road which was quiet as usual. I stood there with the car door open. Dawn finished her fag, gave me a wee wave and went back in the pub. Meanwhile Rocky and Alex came to drunken blows. Alex nearly split his head open on the car door. His dad threw him onto the back seat.

Rocky – Get in there, you dafty cunt, you

Alex – Fuckin' stupid oldy bastard

We eventually set off and I established somehow that Birdie's was in Bellsbank. A mate of theirs, I imagined.

Alex – Stop at the fuckin' Spar, big 'un! We need some booze

I stopped outside the Spar and Alex got out.

Rocky – Where's that wee cunt going?

Me – I think he's getting some booze

Rocky – I'm going in then

Rocky got out the cab and I followed and stood in the doorway of the shop to see if Mike would serve them. An argument erupted in the shop with Rocky threatening violence if they didn't get their booze. Mike caved in and eventually Rocky emerged with a tray of Tennent's and some Buckfast with Alex falling all over the place. He eventually managed to find the car door while Rocky dropped cans all over the pavement. Luckily the bottles were safely on the back seat by then.

Predictably another argument flared and they got quite nasty with each other while I picked up the loose cans and tossed them on the back seat. Eventually we all got in and off we headed for Birdie's. The mile there seemed to last forever as Alex and Rocky swore at each other and threw some quite painful looking punches. Neither of them could give me a specific address, but I was guided to Birdie's house by Alex's shaky pointing and I pulled up outside.

Me – So lads. I guess you won't want tonight's taxi that you booked earlier

Rocky – Eh?

Me – From New Cumnock

Rocky – Aye, we've just fuckin' come back from there on the fuckin' bus

Me – I guessed. So you won't want a taxi tonight then?

Alex – What the fuck you on about, big 'un?

Me – I took you to New Cumnock earlier

Rocky – Aye

Me – You booked a return for midnight... and paid for it too. So you'll want it cancelled and your money back then, I guess

Alex – Eh?

Rocky – What?

Me – Basically guys, I owe you £13.60p

Rocky actually managed to pay for the hire we had just endured with some change from the Spar.

Rocky – You got my fuckin' money?

Me – Calm down, Rocky. I'll just get it now

I counted out the refund of the cancelled hire and plonked it in Rocky's shaky hand. Once they'd collected their booze and got out the car, I was out of there. I radioed Natalie.

Me – TC6 clear in Bellsbank

Natalie – Roger. You're clear for twenty

Me – If either Rocky or Alex phone for a taxi... I'm in Inverness, OK?

Natalie (laughing) – Aye, Roger

Later on I related the tale to Boss. He casually explained that Rocky had done this a few times, and yes he did know where the Brig Inn was.

Same Old Conversation – May 2009

The following story could have taken place any time between March 2008 and July 2011 to be honest. It was a Groundhog Day hire, but May 2009 was the first time I actually realised just how samey they all were.

Donald only ever got a taxi when he couldn't get a lift home for whatever reason... and I usually picked him up around one pm by which time he was annoyingly drunk. Not blootered but just very annoying. He got in the Railway when it opened at eleven am and he shovelled it down his neck for the next couple of hours. I always made extra effort to get him exactly on time too, but could never repeat my "bang on time" feat. Hires had usually gone a bit quiet by one o'clock so it was easy enough to drive the forty or so yards to the Railway, give him the signal and he was out the pub then in the taxi sharpish. A friend whose name I never knew would be with him most of the time.

This was the script. Donald would get in the front and his friend in the back. His friend was a nice guy who never really said much, although I did notice him shake his head a lot at the identical conversation we had every time. Both were fairly ordinary guys in their sixties.

Me – Afternoon, gentlemen

Friend – John, pal

Donald – Always on time as usual

Me – I do my best

Donald – Aye well, that Andy is no fuckin' use. Always late he is. That's why I use your taxis

Me – Andy not very reliable then?

Donald – Useless

Me – Nice to know

I came to the conclusion over the years that folk switched sides between the taxi outfits in the village on very flimsy pretexts a lot of the time. I would imagine that Andy's drivers were just as good as myself when it came to punctuality, and that Donald, like many others, switched to Boss's taxis over issues other than poor timekeeping. I have no doubt that exactly the same conversations happened in Andy's cabs, with Boss or myself or other drivers being the villain.

Donald – How much is this fuckin' taxi anyway, big 'un?

Me – £2.40p, Donald

Donald – I'll give you a wee tip if I've got enough

He would rummage for coins and plonk £3 in my hand.

Me – Cheers, Donald

Donald – No problem, big 'un. Keep the change... you're always on time... I tell them cunts in the pub to phone a taxi for me and they always ask "Andy's?" and I always say "No... Boss"

Me – Fair play, Donald

A wee pause for breath.

Donald – I used to drive buses... Twenty seven fuckin' years I drove buses... don't tell me about fuckin' keeping time

Me – Tricky job I should imagine

Donald – Fuckin' right it is... met some right cunts on there I tell you... I ken who all the wankers are

Me – I bet

By now we're driving up Donald's street where I also lived previously with my then girlfriend before our relationship ended not long after I started cabbing. I moved elsewhere after that.

Donald (pointing to my old house) – That's your old house

Me – Aye

Donald – So why did you move out then? Not that it's any of my business

Me – The missus and I went our separate ways

Donald – Sad that... she was a lovely lassie

Me – Aye Donald, I know

Donald – Still that's life, I suppose

Me – Aye

Donald – So how did you split the money up from the house sale? Not that it's any of my business

Friend – Fuck's sake man, you ask John that same question every time

Donald – Only asking. He can tell me to fuck off if he wants

Thankfully I always arrived at his house by this time.

Me – Here we are, gentlemen

Donald – Oh right. Thanks, big 'un

Friend – Cheers, John

They got out the car quickly. In all the numerous times I had taken this guy home, his conversation didn't vary by more than a sentence or two. The biggest change in dialogue I can recall was this once when he got in the taxi and was raging about some bloke who pissed on his duvet about forty years previously.

You Ken Where I Live - May 2009

Boss took a call late one afternoon while I struggled with yet another tricky level of Gem Drop on my phone. He hung up after a brief chat.

Boss – Go and get Mickey in the square and take the silly old sausage home

Me – OK

I knew who Mickey was. He was a rather burly and sour gentleman who I had taken home just the once not long after I first started back in 2006 and he was a regular face in the local pubs. He was stood at the side of the square and gesticulated at me as I pulled up next to him. He got in.

Me (addressing him politely) – Mr Soandso

Mickey (grumpily and slightly drunk) – Home. And call me Mickey. All this "Mr Soandso" nonsense gets on my nerves

Me – OK. I'm not exactly sure where you live Mickey

Mickey – Of course you fuckin' ken... don't come the cunt, big 'un

Me – I'm not "coming the cunt" Mickey. I don't know where you live

Mickey – For fuck's sake, big 'un you've taken me home before. Get on with it, man. You ken where I live

Me – Mickey. I'm sorry but I don't know where you live

Now I honestly couldn't recall where he lived. I'd taken him home once before about two years previously I vaguely remembered, but how in the hell he could even think I knew where he lived was beyond me.

Mickey – For fuck's sake, you've taken me home before

Me (touching my brow) – Have I? Oh yes I vaguely recall maybe taking you home

Mickey – Perhaps I should fuckin' drive

Me – No sir, you're blootered

Mickey – Look just take me fuckin' home OK? Enough of all this carry on

Me – Just tell me your address, or even a street name, and we're on our way Mickey

Mickey (very bluntly) – Bellsbank

I pulled off and headed for Bellsbank. Eventually I'd get Mickey gesticulating to turn up his street I imagined, but I naughtily decided to ask him at every road we came to along Merrick Drive which forms the spine of the estate. Other roads branched off left and right along its length. The first branch-offs were Auchenroy and Finlas.

Me – Auchenroy? Finlas?

Mickey (unhappy) – No!

The next branch-off was Reicawr which led to four other roads.

Me – Reicawr?

Mickey (very unhappy) – No, for fuck's sake!

Me – Corserine? Minnoch?

Mickey (seriously fed up by now) – Fuckin' no, big 'un!

Me – Macaterick? Hillcrest?

Mickey (really grumpy and pissed off now) – No! Fuckin' no!

I passed the end of Reicawr and drove by safe in the knowledge I'd eliminated it and the four roads that led off it. Before we got to the next branch-off Mickey caved in.

Mickey – Soandso Street, big 'un, for fuck's sake. OK?

Me – Excellent, we're nearly there

I drove on and turned into Soandso Street

Me – Number, Mickey?

Mickey – I'll tell you when to stop. You've brought me here before

Me – Apologies for not having a brilliant memory, Mickey

Mickey – Stop here!

I stopped and he handed me the exact fare then got out. I committed his address to memory. Now I occasionally had folk in the cab who honestly couldn't give me a house number where they were going or even the street sometimes and I didn't mind. They knew where they wanted to go but didn't know the proper address. I imagine a lot of people couldn't name their mates' addresses, for example. I've got a few friends and I couldn't tell you all of their addresses. But surely if a cabbie asks your address it would be wise to just tell them, I would think.

The New Cabbie – June 2009

Bruce, a quietly-spoken guy in his sixties, had worked for Boss for a while, delivering parcels in the Cumnocks, but it came to a point when Boss had to take some time out of driving as much as he used to. Bruce already had a local PHV badge so he started driving a taxi to help out while Boss was unavailable.

He opted to cover weekday evenings. He would do his short parcel round in the morning and be home by noon. I would do weekday daytimes and we'd both muck in to cover weekends for the next few weeks until Boss could return to the fold. The school kid runs were our absolute priority, and Boss, myself and another of Boss's drivers, Geoff, continued to do those as usual. Boss put me "in charge" in his absence though.

Bruce lived in Dalmellington but he didn't know it like the back of his hand unlike Boss and myself. Therefore he didn't know certain characters or our regulars, and they didn't know him either. It was coming up to six pm on the first day of these new arrangements, and I'd just given the phone to Bruce so he could cover the evening shift. The phone rang and he answered it. I could hear the entire conversation as the phone was very loud.

Bruce – Hello, T&C Taxis

Caller – Er... is that the taxis?

Bruce – Yes

Caller – Is Boss or John there?

Bruce (looking at me and I shook my head) – No

Caller – Oh

Bruce – You want a taxi?

Caller – Er... yes

Bruce – OK then, where are you, where are you going, when do you want it and what's your name?

Caller – Eh? Boss or John usually just come for me

Bruce – Well they know who you are, where you are and probably have a good idea where you're going. I don't. I'm new

Caller – Oh... I'm in Bellsbank

Bellsbank consists of hundreds of houses and flats in fourteen streets.

Bruce – No good to me, I'm afraid. Where are you in Bellsbank?

The caller gave Bruce a road name.

Bruce – Well, that narrows it down. House number?

Caller – I'll call back

I hung on for a minute or so and made a coffee. Bruce and I had a wee chat, and I then decided to stay on a few more hours and take charge of the office and radio. The phone rang again.

Bruce – Hello, T&C Taxis

Caller – Yeah, I'm at number eighteen

Bruce – Who's at number eighteen? Where?

Caller – What do you mean?

Bruce – You're at eighteen you say... what does that mean?

Caller – I called you a minute ago

Bruce – Oh you're the lady from Suchandsuch Road, I take it. We get a few calls here you know

Caller – Right, I'm at eighteen Suchandsuch

Bruce – OK... where are you going?

Caller – Jeezo... down the street

"Down the street" is a commonly used local term for journeys to the middle of Dalmellington. But I had "down the street" for journeys to half a dozen different places in the village and down to the next village too which is miles away.

Bruce – OK, you want a taxi now, I take it?

Caller – Yes

Bruce gave up trying to get a name and destination. I whispered to him where I think she'd be going and wrote her name on the booking sheet.

Bruce – OK, I'll be there in a few minutes

Caller – OK, then

The call ended and I took the phone and told Bruce I'd control things from the office and shout him on the radio.

Now this was pretty typical of folk in a wee village who get the same few taxi drivers every time they call. They're lucky in a way they live in a village where the cabbies virtually knew everyone. I actually think Boss did know everyone, and who they were related to and so on.

The problem was when a new guy like Bruce started cabbing or the hassle I had when I started. Although in my favour, I wasn't answering the phone until I'd done a few months and had learned almost all of the "regulars" and "characters".

Typical calls would run like these select examples.

Mr B always asked, "First available?"

Mrs R just said, "Shops and back."

Mr T just said, "When can I get a taxi, big 'un?"

Mr G who we got messages for always said, "I got a list here... messages... whenever you can fit me in... no rush... you ken where I am."

And so on. I could tell as soon as I saw the name on the phone as it rang what the hire would be. Bruce hadn't a clue who they were, where they were, or where they might be going. However even I got unstuck sometimes as the following tale illustrates perfectly.

Down The Street – June 2009

The phone rang this one day and it was the young lad who worked at the Co-op.

Youth – Can we have a taxi here for a lady?

Me – Aye

I could see it was the Co-op from the phone display.

Me – You want it now?

Youth – Aye

Me – OK, I can just about squeeze it in. I've got a hire in five minutes. Where they going?

Youth – Just down the street

Me – OK, I'll be there in a few minutes

Now I thought it would either be Mrs B or Mrs P or Mrs H all of whom got us regularly from the Co-op so I didn't ask the name. I'll know when I see them. I got there and it was a senior lady I'd never seen before and never saw again either. I placed her messages in the boot and we got in the car. She gave me her name and I wrote it on the booking sheet.

Me – Where do you want to go madam?

Lady – Dalharco Avenue

Me (slightly shocked and a wee bit annoyed) – Patna!

Lady – Yes. Is that OK?

Me (thinking no it's not OK really) – Yes, that's fine

Patna is five miles down the A713 not "down the street" but I took the hire on and it wasn't the lady's fault. So I headed off as briskly as common sense and the law would allow down to Patna, dropped the lady off, then headed back sharpish and spent the next few hires being ten minutes late until I could claw the time back. From that day onwards, the phrase "down the street" meant nothing to me and I insisted on a proper destination. Another lesson learned.

Runaround – August 2009

Jerry and his wife Fiona were two of the nicest people I ever met and although they loved each other very much, they had moments of tension like all couples experience from time to time. They were retired, had a good group of friends and led active social lives. They used Boss's taxis frequently and I would often get a call on Sundays to either take one or both of them to a pub or their home. One warm Sunday afternoon as I took charge of things while Boss took a day off, the phone rang and Fiona gave me her usual opening line as soon as I picked up.

Fiona (whispering) – Taxi now John, please. I'm two doors down from my house hiding behind a blue car. Quick as you can but don't toot your horn

Me – Righto, Fiona. There in a jiffy

I drove up to Bellsbank and as I pulled up quietly two doors down from her house, she sprang out, jumped in the car and squashed down in the front seat to hide below the windows.

Fiona – Go, go, go!

I pulled away and after a few yards she sat upright and put the seatbelt on.

Me – Good afternoon, Fiona

Fiona – Aye, it will be now I've managed to escape the house without waking him up. I needed to get out. He was driving me nuts today

Me – Where to Fiona?

Fiona – Peggy's. If Jerry phones up asking for me, you don't ken where I am. OK?

Me – I wouldn't tell him anyway Fiona. It would be against the law

Fiona – Tell him I've gone to Ayr or something

I dropped Fiona off at Peggy's then returned to the office to give my coffee another trip in the microwave. A while later the phone rang. It was Jerry.

Me – Hello, T&C Taxis

Jerry – It's Jerry. I need a taxi to Boyd's Bar

Me – I'll be up in five minutes, Jerry

Jerry – Thanks, big 'un

I pulled up outside Jerry's, he got in and we were soon on the short trip to Boyd's Bar.

Jerry – You seen Fiona about?

Me – You mean in the village? I haven't seen her. No

Jerry – You ken what I mean, laddie. In the fuckin' taxi. You taken her anywhere today?

Me – I couldn't say, sir

Jerry – Don't come the cunt with me, big 'un

Me – Jerry you know I couldn't tell you if I'd taken your wife anywhere in the taxi

Jerry – Fuck's sake, man

Me – Hey listen. If you went somewhere, would you want me to tell Fiona?

Jerry – No I suppose not

Me – If I'd taken her to hospital then of course I'd tell you, but otherwise I'm saying fuck all, mate. Can you imagine the shit I'd get off Boss and Fiona herself and everyone else if they knew I'd done that? No way, Jerry. Sorry

Jerry – Aye, you're right, big 'un

I dropped him at Boyd's and headed back to the office. The phone rang.

Me – Hello, T&C Taxis

Fiona – I need a taxi to Patna, John. I'm at Peggy's

Me – I'll be there in two minutes

I collected Fiona from Peggy's and took her to Patna. A short while later I got a call from Boyd's Bar and I soon took Jerry to the Railway. Then he went to the Running Dog in Burnton. This carried on all afternoon with me running both of them to nearly every pub in the Dalmellington area in a huge game of cat and mouse, until Boss appeared around 5 pm and took over. He ran through the hire sheet and cashed me in.

Boss – Well, they nearly broke the record

Me – Eh?

Boss – Fiona and Jerry. I see you had them eleven times today

Me – Aye, something like that

Boss – I had them about fifteen times this one day a while ago

And I thought eleven would have been some kind of record.

Play on the Radio – October 2009

I was sat in the office at around eleven o'clock this one weekday morning and we got a call from Sue, a young lady in her twenties who used us fairly regularly. She wanted her usual hire which was basically a trip from her place down to the chemist in the square then back home. A hire I did at least once or twice a week. Boss sent me while he attended to some paperwork that I was now convinced he was inventing himself. I think the United Nations runs on less paperwork.

She came out the house in her pyjamas and got in the car, texting non-stop. I drove off. I've seen her in her jammies before so I wasn't bothered at all. I was listening to a comedy play on Radio 4 and I'd only driven about four hundred yards or so.

Sue – Is that noise from the radio?

Me (not really getting what she means) – What noise?

Sue (pointing at the car radio) – That

Me – It's a play... a comedy

Sue (amazed) – A play! On the radio?

Me – Er... yes

Sue – I thought it was just music and news on the radio

Me – Er... No, plays, sport... all sorts really

Sue – Oh I didn't ken that

So I dropped her off back home after her visit to the chemist and shouted on the radio.

Me – TC6 clear in Bellsbank

Boss – Hire in the office up to Bellsbank

Me – Roger, on my way

I got back to the office still in a wee bit of shock.

Me (radio) – TC6 outside

Boss – Aye, it's Dean walking out the door just now

I recognised the guy immediately as he ambled out the office, and over to the car. He was a fairly ordinary bloke in his thirties.

Me – Hi, Dean. How you doing? Keeping well?

Dean – Aye, I'm fine John thanks. You?

Me – Aye, I'm OK mate. Just had an interesting question from a customer which astonished me a bit really

Dean – Oh yes. What was that then?

Dean fastened his seatbelt and I set off.

Me – Well they asked me what that noise was coming out the radio

Dean – What? You mean that talking and laughing I can hear on there now?

Me – Aye

Dean – What did you say?

Me – I said it was just a play and she seemed amazed that there are plays on the radio

Dean – Er... what's a play?

I honestly can't remember what I said because I was so astonished by his question as well as the one from the previous customer.

Lies – November 2009

Higgy was a young man in his early twenties who used our taxis fairly regularly, as did the rest of his family. He staggered into the taxi office at around 9.30 this one morning not long after we'd all returned from doing the school runs. He held onto the door for dear life.

Higgy – Taxi please, Boss... I'm fucked

Boss – Aye, Higgy. John will take you now

Me – Aye, come on, Higgy

Higgy – Thanks, John

We got in the taxi and I moved off heading for Higgy's place where he lived with his parents and girlfriend.

Higgy – Aye, I'm fucked, John

Me – Rough night, mate?

Higgy – No, I've just had some Valium and a wee bit of something else. But I'm clean now and off the hard stuff

Me – OK, cool

Never having taken drugs myself, except for cigarettes and the occasional drink, I never really knew which drugs were hard or soft to be honest. I tried some "waccy baccy" once many years ago and it made me ill, and I also tried some amyl nitrate which sent me insane for a minute or so. That put me off substances really, and I've never bothered with any of them since. Even a couple of beers would knock me out cold, and in the years I drove a taxi, I never drank at all for fear of being ill, or something untoward happening.

Higgy – Aye, I'm off the cocaine and all that shit now... cuz of the wee 'un

Me – How is the wee lassie?

Higgy – No fuckin' idea, pal... them cunts at the social took her off us... they think we're bad parents

Me – Terrible

Higgy – Aye... I told the cunt there that he should try coming off hard drugs and that methadone is fuckin' shit anyway... told the cunt that it's like drinking cough medicine

By now we were approaching his flat where he stayed, but he'd been texting on his mobile while chatting to me, and not looking where we were going really.

Me – Nearly home, Higgy

Higgy (looking up) – Fuckin' hell, John don't take me home! My dad will kill me if he sees me in this state and I'm supposed to be going straight. Take me up to S's place please, pal. I'll dry out a bit there

Luckily "S" lived just one street further along so I hadn't gone completely the wrong direction. Higgy ducked down as I drove past his place, then we safely turned the corner into "S's" road and I pulled up. Higgy paid me and he tottered off.

Oh I should mention that "S" was a provider of substances to certain folks in the area. I think Higgy may have told me a wee fib about being off substances. I never saw the guy straight.

A Foot Of Snow – December 2009

The snow on 22nd December 2009 in the Doon Valley turned absolutely atrocious in a matter of minutes it seemed. No snow at all until the morning then it came down hard and stuck like glue. The gritting trucks and snowploughs got stuck in Ayr and couldn't get up the A713 along the Doon Valley. I was "lucky" enough to get into work at seven thirty am before the roads got too bad then it snowed like the end of the world. The schools closed and we then struggled to take the kids home that we had not long ago taken into school. The roads were like skating rinks. Then the three buses an hour stopped. It just got worse and worse as the day wore on.

They were the worst driving conditions I'd ever encountered in my life but I never mentioned it because as a Brummie, Boss and the rest would probably have laughed at my southern softness. It got so bad that I eventually did mention the appalling weather and Boss agreed, saying it was the worst weather he could remember and he'd driven trucks and taxis all his life. The sooner this day ended the better and I dreaded every coming minute.

Some people never seem to notice anything however.

I had the taxi mobile while Boss went off on a long hire somewhere. It rang and I answered it on my earpiece so I hadn't a clue who was calling. The phone itself was in my pocket.

Me – Hello, T&C Taxis

Madge – Ooh hello, is that you John?

Me (recognising her voice) – Hi Madge

Madge – I need a taxi, John

Me – You need it soon, Madge? You at home?

Madge – Aye

Me – Madge, the roads are very bad today and you live up a bit of a hill there in Other Road. I'll try and get to you but you may have to meet me at the bottom of your road

Madge – Ooh, is it really that bad, John?

Me – Yes, Madge the roads are very bad

Madge – Ooh

Me – I'll just finish this hire I'm doing then I'll try and get to you. I'll phone you if I can't get up your road. OK?

Madge – Er, OK John

So I finished the hire I had and aimed the taxi in the general direction of Madge's house. Madge was a lady in her forties who used our taxi services regularly. Sometimes her boyfriend Steve would come along too. I could not get up her road so I parked up, called her and got no reply. I trudged the fifty or so yards up her road and knocked on her door. She scurried out "oohing" and "aahing" at all the snow everywhere. It still fell heavily from the black sky.

Madge – Ooh, there's a lot of snow, John

Me – Yes Madge, I'd noticed

Madge – Ooh, where's the taxi, John?

Me – Bottom of the street, Madge. I couldn't get up here. The snow is terrible

Madge – Ooh

Me – Ah well Madge, it's downhill to the taxi from here anyway. What's Steve up to today?

Madge – Watching telly

Me – Wise man

We walked down the hill to the taxi. I saw a freshly abandoned car and figured that it wouldn't be long before the entire village was the world's messiest car park. We got in the taxi and were soon crawling down to the Keystore in Dalmellington. We arrived and she shot out and into the shop. She got back in the taxi about two minutes later with a wee bag of messages.

Me – Home, Madge? Or your brother's place?

Madge – Home

Me – Now have you got everything you need?

Madge – Yes

Me – OK then. We're off

I learned always to ask Madge, and certain other folks, if they wanted destinations other than "home". It wasn't a problem if they wanted somewhere else because I could easily drive from one end of the village to the other in minutes anyway, excepting the current weather conditions. I just didn't want to drive in the totally opposite direction. Off we crawled through the falling snow and chaos. Despite the fact that people were pushing cars, lots of folks were slipping over on their bottoms and the local kids took to peppering cars with snowballs, Madge failed to notice any of it. Eventually after some slipping and sliding I pulled up where I had parked before at the bottom of her road.

Me – Well Madge, that's as far as I can get you

Madge – OK

Me – You want a hand walking up the brae?

Madge – No it's OK, John

She paid me and I slid off back towards the taxi office for a coffee. Later that morning about noonish, Boss was back in the office doing some paperwork and shouted me over the radio. I was technically in control as I still had the phone.

Boss – TC6, what's your position?

Me – Just finishing one off in a minute or two at the square, TC1

Boss – There's a young lady in the office needing a taxi up to Other Road

Me – Be there in a minute or so but tell them I can't get up Other Road. I can drop them off at the bottom if that's OK and I'll carry their bags up if they have any

Boss – Roger

I thought to myself it may be Mrs C or even Mrs G. Either way I envisaged helping them on foot up Other Road with their messages. I dropped my hire off in the square and slid the few yards to the taxi office. I walked in to relay a verbal message to Boss, and there was Madge sat on one of our luxuriously upholstered sofas with another wee bag of messages in her lap. She'd obviously forgotten something and walked down to the village and didn't fancy the walk home in the still falling snow.

Me – Hi Madge

Madge – Hello John

Me – Taxi home?

Madge – Yes please, John

She followed me out the office into the gloom and snow and we got in my taxi.

Me – So Madge, have you got everything this time?

Madge (showing me her bag) – Yes, sorry John

Me – Hey, it's no concern of mine really Madge. You can get as many taxis as you want. I'm just saying the roads are bad, I can't get up Other Road and I don't want you slipping on these pavements. The roads are getting worse too

Madge – OK

We set off and I was soon crawling past the Keystore in Main Street.

Me – Not wanting anything from the Keystore then?

Madge – No

Me (light-heartedly) – You sure, Madge?

Madge – Aye

I eventually dropped Madge off at the bottom of her road, and I got on with some other hires.

A while later, I sent Boss off to Ayr with a good regular and he laughingly told me he'd be back sometime this year probably. He also told me to use my common sense about which roads and hills I could get up. By this point, I'd given up any attempts at getting along a good number of roads in both Dalmellington and Bellsbank. He told me to just stop taking anyone, anywhere if it got too bad.

About four in the afternoon it was getting very dark, and the snow fell on the still ungritted skating rinks that passed for roads. Cars littered the streets and I had seen a few close shaves, and one bus all day instead of three an hour. I was thinking of calling a halt to all hires when I got a regular up to Bellsbank. They're good folk so I struggled up the brae then along Merrick Drive to drop them at the bottom of their road. I was heading back to the office for a much needed microwaved coffee when the phone rang.

Me – Hello, T&C Taxis

Madge – Hello John, can I have a taxi please?

Most folk had not even ventured outside so I'd been fairly quiet, but I didn't like letting people down if they needed a taxi and I could pick her up on the way back to the office from where I was easily enough.

Me – Certainly, Madge. I'll be at the bottom of your road in about three minutes. OK? See you there

Madge – OK

Three minutes later I pulled up at the bottom of Other Road and predictably there was no sign of Madge so I trudged up to her house once again, and pretty soon we were in the taxi again crawling and sliding down to Dalmellington.

Me – Where to Madge?

Madge – Shop

Me – Now Madge, there's a few shops in the village... which one do you need? Keystore?

Madge – Sorry, John. Yes, the Keystore

Me – OK. Then where to? Your brother's place?

Madge – Home

I slid up to the Keystore and Madge was out then back in the taxi like a bullet. I glanced at the wee bag in her hand, but couldn't make out what was in there. It was no business of mine anyway, but I'm a nosey sausage and the roads were so bad now I decided that this would be my last hire of the day.

Me – Got everything, Madge?

Madge – Yes

Me – Now Madge, are you sure because the weather is getting worse and the roads are now really very bad indeed. I won't be able to come out for you again in these conditions. You understand?

Madge – Yes

Me (pressing home the message) – You don't need milk or tea bags or bread or fags or ...

Basically I listed everything possible she might want.

Me – ... booze?

Madge (holding up the bag) – No, I just got booze. I forgot it before

Me – No bother then, Madge. Home it is

I took her to the bottom of the ski jump that passed for her street and slid back to the office. I had a relaxing coffee and cigarette while I waited for Boss to return. He shouted me over the radio as he came back into range much later than he normally would after a run to Ayr and back.

Boss – TC1 back in the village

Me – Aye TC1, I'm in the office. I'll put the kettle on

Boss – Good, I'm parched

Me – What's the A713 like?

Boss – Passable with care but I think we're done for the day

Boss got back to the office and I handed him a tea in his favourite chipped mug. I told him I'd had Madge in the taxi again and I bet she'd want another at some point.

Boss – Not in this weather, John. Cash in. Fuck off. I'm done

I cashed in and slid home in my own car. I think Boss had an evening in front of the television and I think Madge phoned again but the call went unanswered.

Local Oaf on Xmas Day – December 2009

One of the local oafs who didn't use taxis much but I knew him because he was a local character, phoned up on Christmas Day about 4 pm or thereabouts. I'd done very little all day except the occasional hire or play Gem Drop. I worked five consecutive Christmas Days my whole time in the job, and every one of them was quiet and peaceful. I didn't mind, and Boss didn't like to leave the village unattended. He tended to work the New Year period himself which was surprisingly quiet also.

The office mobile rang and it just displayed a number with no name so I knew it wasn't a regular and answered it.

Me – Hello, T&C Taxis

Oaf – I need a taxi

I recognised his voice immediately.

Me – Planning on starting your own taxi outfit are we, sir?

Oaf – Aye, very funny, big 'un. I need a taxi

Me – OK, where are you?

Oaf – Boyd's Bar in Bellsbank, I'm outside. It's fuckin' shut

Me – Where do you want to go?

Oaf – Down the street

Me – That means fuck all to me. Where do you want to go?

Oaf – Fuck's sake, John. The Masons

Me – OK, I'll be up in a few minutes. OK?

Oaf – Aye, hurry up man, it's fuckin' freezing here

I locked up the office, drove through the deserted centre of Dalmellington then up the brae to Bellsbank. The busier roads in the village had cleared considerably in the past three days, and I was soon enjoying the company of Oaf on a Christmas Day.

Me – Afternoon, sir

Oaf – Hi, John. What you been up to?

Me – Oh not a lot. Playing games on my phone. You been up to much today?

Oaf – Nah. Done fuck all. Just want to see what's going on in the village. Fuckin Boyd's is shut, man

Me – Well, it is Christmas Day, sir. Masons Club then, sir?

Oaf – Aye

Soon we arrived at the totally deserted and dark and obviously closed Masons Club.

Me – Here we are, sir

Oaf – It's fuckin' closed, man

Me – Oh yes so it is. Well, it is Christmas Day, sir

Oaf – Fuck's sake. Can you take me to the Spar?

Me – Certainly, sir

I pulled away, arriving a minute later outside the deserted and dark and obviously closed Spar.

Me – Here we are, sir

Oaf – It's fuckin' closed, man

Me – Oh yes so it is. Well it is Christmas Day, sir

Oaf – Fuck's sake. Can you take me to the Black Bull?

Me – Certainly, sir

I pulled away knowing that the Bull was shut as was everywhere else in the village. I also knew that Oaf's journey would end at the Bull because I would park up outside and walk directly over the road to the taxi office. Within seconds we were round the corner and I stopped outside the Black Bull, applied the handbrake and turned off the ignition. Oaf paid me and I opened the door and got out.

Me – Here we are, sir

Oaf (getting out the car) – It's fuckin' closed, man

Me – Oh yes so it is. Well it is Christmas Day, sir

Oaf – What the fuck am I supposed to do now? Does anybody fuckin' work on Christmas Day around here?

Me – I'm going in that taxi office over there to microwave my coffee and play Gem Drop. It's Christmas fuckin' Day for Pete's sake. Nowhere is fuckin' open. You know how many people in this village are working today?

Oaf – No

Me – One

Oaf – Who's that?

Me – Me you dopey cunt! Now get to fuck

Oaf pulled a face and slumped off into the gathering gloom.

Library – January 2010

I got a call one day soon after New Year from someone I'd never picked up before. The busier roads were fairly clear, but snow still lay thick everywhere else and conditions underfoot were not good to say the least. I'd done hardly any hires all day once the morning school kid runs were done. I think most folks had wisely opted to stay in again.

Me – Hello, T&C Taxis

Lady caller – I need a taxi for Mr N to take him up the library

Me – OK, no problem. Where does Mr N live and what time does he want the taxi?

Lady caller – Eh?

Now this was typical of a lot of folks. I knew all our regulars, where they lived, where they would probably want to go, and could hazard a guess at what time they'd want picking up too. But a new caller was different.

Me – Where does Mr N want picking up from?

She gave me the address.

Me – What time?

Lady caller – Oh... Er... Two o'clock is fine

Me – OK, I'll get him then... bye

Lady caller – OK, bye

At just before two pm I went to get Mr N and pulled up at the end of his path. He tottered and slipped despite holding on to the railing that ran the length of his path. I got out to offer assistance as I did to anyone in the current weather conditions, but especially to a frail looking man such as Mr N, and we took a while crawling through the snow to the car. He also had a couple of library books with him which I took care of under one arm while he held onto my other.

Eventually we got to the library around ten past two, and I could almost smell my coffee which needed another trip in the microwave. Thick snow lay everywhere. I told Mr N the fare and he paid me.

Mr N – Now can you come and get me in... ooh... about half an hour?

Me (making a show of looking at my booking sheet) – Er... Afraid not Mr N... two thirty any good? That's twenty minutes away

Mr N – Not really, I've got these books to sort out... and get some more

Me – I've got to get off to Patna to pick up school kids at three

Mr N – Oh... Andy's driver normally just comes to get me

This happened now and then as well. Andy's taxi company didn't do school kid runs. Some of the locals thought we were the same taxi company too probably. It also explained why the lady caller wasn't very clear on the phone. She either thought I drove for Andy despite the fact she had to dial our number to get me, or she was under the false impression that both taxi outfits operated in exactly the same manner. School kid runs were our absolute priority and nothing could interfere with them and cause us to be late. I also wondered why she phoned us instead of Andy. I assumed the weather had some impact on his inability to take Mr N that day.

Me – Well I drive for Boss so I don't know how Andy runs his business, but I can't get you any later than half two and that would need to be sharp because I have to get off to Patna for my school kid runs

Mr N – I'll come to your office then

Me – There's only myself working today. No-one in the office I'm afraid

Mr N – Can I phone up?

Me – Sure, but I've got the phone and I'll be away in Patna and won't get back here until three thirty at the earliest

Mr N thought while I looked at the thick snow all around and tried to smell my coffee back at the office next door.

Mr N – I'll go to your office when I'm done here and wait

Me – There's no-one in the office today. There's just me on duty. The office is locked and Boss and our other drivers will be off doing their own school kid runs. I'm in control today

Mr N – Oh...

I could see Mr N was in a bit of an awkward situation.

Me – Actually the best option for you right now is forget returning those books and I take you home

Mr N – They're due and I've read them and I need to exchange them. No, that's no good. I need the library now

Me – Sorry sir, but I don't see any alternative

Mr N – But I need to change these books

The situation struck me as ridiculous. I could appreciate the guy wanting to change his library books, but the circumstances he now faced made that a nonsensical option in my eyes. I did not want to see him stuck with no obvious means of getting home.

Me – I'll take you home for nothing now, sir, and I'll pick you up after the school runs and bring you back here

Mr N – No. No good I'm afraid

And with that he just got out the car and I helped him inch his way to the library.

Now if the lady caller had been clearer on the phone in the first place and explained that he wanted to get home after thirty minutes, I would have explained all this to her and maybe picked the guy up earlier so I could get him home before the school runs. Instead she made assumptions which probably caused Mr N a deal of inconvenience. I never did see Mr N for a hire later that day or any time afterwards either.

If it hadn't been for the school kid runs I simply had to do, I would have bent over backwards to help the guy out because I felt bad about him being left in that situation. Doubtlessly our name was mud afterwards because we left Mr N at the library with no obvious way of getting home, but at least his library books were returned on time I suppose. If it was me I'd have taken one look outside and thought to myself, "I'm staying in... overdue library book or not."

Uruguay – January 2010

The atrocious weather conditions showed no sign of easing off whatsoever, and another fun day sliding about the village in my taxi beckoned. The phone rang and I knew immediately that the caller, Bev, lived on a stretch of road I could get to easily enough, and that she usually went to a place on an equally easy bit of road for the weather conditions. No hills equalled a nice easy hire. Bev was a very regular customer and we'd known each other for a while now. A lady in her thirties with a husband and two kids. I drove to her house and she jumped in the car, thrusting her hands onto the hot air blowers. I turned them up to full.

Bev – Ooh, John I'm sick of this bloody snow

Me – Aye. I'm thinking of emigrating. I'm fed up of the snow and cold and sliding around in this car all day long

Bev (laughing) – Good idea, John... Where would you go?

Me (after a wee think) – Uruguay, I reckon

I think I'd watched something on the TV about Uruguay a few days before, and it was the first country that came to mind.

Bev – What?

Me – Uruguay

Bev – Never heard of it. What's Youraguy?

She pronounced it very badly. Now I thought that she meant she didn't know *where* it was... I had the radio on and the heater fans were quite loud too.

Me – Between Brazil and Argentina

Bev – You're making this up

Me – Making what up?

Bev – This fuckin' Youraguy

Me – You've lost me Bev ... Making it up? I dunno what you mean

Bev – There's no such place

Me (astonished) – You mean you've never heard of it?

Bev – You just made it up

Me – Honestly. It's between Brazil and Argentina. The capital city is Montevideo. Only a wee place

Bev (laughing) – Oh good one... "Monty Video"

Me – I can't believe you've never heard of it

Bev (slightly annoyed now) – Well I haven't... and I don't believe you

The rest of the journey passed in silence because I was a bit astonished that Bev had never heard of Uruguay, and she was probably annoyed with me for making a country up that didn't exist.

Yes I Do Remember Where You Live, Sir – January 2010

The snow lay on the roads for day after day with the odd fresh fall adding to it throughout January 2010. It stayed the same level of atrociousness if there's such a word. Certain hills got easier to scale, but a lot didn't. Mickey phoned for a taxi from Peggy's and I pulled up outside the pub as he exited. He soon got in the front seat, with a friend of his getting in the back. His friend, the jolly nice Mr K, didn't live up a hilly road and I could get him home no problem. Mickey's road was still impassable however. I could remember where he lived though, having burned it into my memory when I took him home before.

Me – Hello Mickey... Mr K

Mickey – Big 'un

Mr K – Hi John

Me – Home, Mickey?

Mickey – Aye

Me – Home, Mr K?

Mr K – Aye John, please

Me – Well I'll give it a go but I've tried and failed a few times so far to get up your street, Mickey. I'll get you home Mr K, no bother

Mr K – Aye, it's flat where I am

Mickey – What? Don't talk daft, man. I've seen other folk getting up my street

Me – Well they must be fantastic drivers or have four-wheel drive

Mickey – No. Ordinary folk in ordinary cars

Mr K tittered in the back as we drove up to Bellsbank while Mickey explained how many folk had managed to scale Soandso Street since 22nd December.

We got to Mickey's road and eventually came to a halt about a third of the way up. Actually I didn't really try that hard, to be honest. Mickey lived near the top of the road, but it wasn't the ascent that worried me, but the descent. I could have struggled up to his house, but then I'd have to turn round and crawl down even further or crawl backwards downhill.

Me – Far as we can get I'm afraid, Mickey

Now I was expecting a barrage of silly nonsense from him as he plonked the fare in my hand.

Mickey – Oh well you did your best. Thanks... bye.

And out he got to trudge the remaining few yards to his house. I turned to Mr K.

Me – I was expecting a bit more abuse than that

Mr K – Aye... I was too

I slid back down Soandso Street onto Merrick Drive and took Mr K home and reflected that perhaps Mickey wasn't so tiresome after all.

Fifteen Minutes – January 2010

Mr C phoned up one morning and he wanted a taxi at two thirty-five. He was very specific about the time too.

Me – Hello, T&C Taxis

Mr C – Oh hello John, it's Mr C. The missus needs a taxi at two thirty-five down to the surgery

I knew without looking at my booking sheet that I had a hire at half past two and directly after that I had to get off and pick school kids up in Patna. I couldn't even squeeze Mr C's missus in as the half two hire finished nowhere near her house, and Patna is in the other direction. Also his missus was very unsteady on her feet and took a while to walk down their path and there was still a wee bit of snow and ice underfoot. And on top of all that, there was NO WAY that we were allowed to be late picking up school kids.

Me – Sorry Mr C, I can't do two thirty-five but I could get you at two twenty

Mr C (after a brief chat with his missus) – That's a bit early, John

Me – Oh... what time is the appointment? I'll do some maths with the timings

Mr C (after another chat with his missus) – Two-forty

Me – Two-twenty then? Any good?

Mr C – Hmm... Two-thirty? Andy's taxis can't pick the missus up at all. He's got something on then

Mr C was a taxi user who partook of both taxi companies in the village, but he appeared to be lumbered with just one choice today.

Me – I'm sorry I can't do two-thirty Mr C... I've got a hire at that time then I'm off to pick up school kids in Patna

Mr C – Two-forty then and I'll phone the surgery and tell them we'll be a few minutes late

Me – I'll be on my way to Patna by then to get school kids

Mr C – School kids?

Me (sarcasm mode) – Yes, Mr C... Small people who go to school

Mr C (getting my sarcasm) – Ooh sorry, John... I thought the schools were closed with the bad weather

Me – Sadly not, Mr C. They're back open

Mr C – So you can't do two thirty-five then?

Me – No sorry, Mr C. Two-twenty and I can get Mrs C then easily. Get to the surgery at two twenty-five. Fifteen minute wait until two-forty for your wife's appointment. Sorted

Mr C – Nah, that's way too early, John. OK, never mind. We'll cancel the appointment. Thanks anyway

And that was that. Cancelling an appointment for the sake of a fifteen minute wait in the surgery didn't seem the obvious choice to me but there you go.

Red Snow – February 2010

The roads had started to clear, but the paths and gardens and rooftops and fields and everywhere else still had a few inches of thick snow that hadn't thawed much. The temperature had hovered around the -5C mark for days on end. I took a hire to Cumnock one morning and on my way back to Dalmellington I turned off the A76 at the Skerrington Roundabout down a wee lane I often used that ran through the opencast coal mine and shaved a few miles and minutes off the journey. As soon as I turned into the lane, I gave my windscreen squirters a quick flick to remove the salt that had built up, but the jets had frozen and the salt smeared over the glass removing all visibility.

There was a wee dirt lay-by just on my left so I pulled in, turned the wipers on and decided to throw some snow on the screen which would remove the salt. I got out the car, bent down and scooped a nice looking lump of snow... which suddenly turned red... then my fingers started tingling. I pulled my hand out and shook the red snow off. Blood poured from several deep cuts in every fingertip bar the wee finger. Oh dear. The low temperature seemingly minimised the pain but blood just kept leaking out my freezing digits and I stepped quickly to the boot of the car and popped it up. I grabbed my dipstick wiping rag and wound it round the three red fingers.

I returned to the lump of red snow and inspected it with my boot, flicking the snow away from what I thought would be a very sharp thistle or something similar. What I found shocked me and made me wonder about the sanity of some people.

Two broken beer glasses full of broken glass. The nearest buildings were a wee housing estate over the other side of the A76. On this side there were just fields for miles with the occasional farm and the opencast mine. Someone must have walked or driven here and deliberately placed them where they sat in this dirt lay-by. Then the heavy snow covered them up.

I cleared the windscreen and drove the fifteen miles back to the office with my right hand hanging out the window. The only rag I had was solid red and dripping but I didn't want to get blood all over the car. My hand was absolutely frozen stiff and started to hurt so I then shook the rag off and jammed my frozen hand under my jumper. I looked a right mess by the time I got back and walked in the office. I obviously went down the surgery right away once I'd shown Boss my very sorry looking red hand.

I got some jabs off the nurse and a lovely bandage. My fingers stung for ages afterwards until they finally eased. Thankfully there was no serious damage so I returned to driving after an hour or so and told various passengers for the next few days that I'd encountered a very sharp bogie. I don't like snow. Especially red snow.

Rab to Maybole – March 2010

Natalie took a call one Saturday morning on behalf of a senior gentleman called Rab we knew quite well. She told the caller the hire would cost £18 and I was sent to pick him up from his nursing home at ten thirty am and take him to Maybole. Thankfully the snow in that winter of 2009/10 had gone and the roads were now back to normal.

I arrived at the home at the appropriate time and pretty soon Rab appeared with a carer, and he looked a wee bit drunk to me. He tottered towards the car. I got out and opened the rear door where he normally sat, and he slid in the back seat then I belted him in.

Me (to his carer) – Is he drunk or poorly?

Carer – Who knows?

She went back in the home and I got in the car and set off. Maybole is a good thirty minute drive away and Rab was asleep by the time we got to Patna which was a bit of a relief actually because I couldn't follow anything he was saying. I took the B742 through Dalrymple and soon arrived in Maybole.

I woke Rab up and asked him where he wanted to go. He roughly articulated he wanted to be near to the cafe at the top of the High Street so I parked up in a suitable spot and walked round to open his door. He'd nodded off again.

Me – Rab... We're here, buddy

Rab (waking) – burp wazzap burp, big 'un, wazzap burp etc, etc

So after a wee struggle he got out the car after taking my arm, and swayed on the pavement. He got his wallet out with difficulty and opened it up.

Rab – Only got a tenner, pal

Me – Oh that's £8 short, Rab

I wasn't angry or fed up at this point. I'd just take the tenner and he could owe us the rest. I then thought I'd not take anything off him. I didn't want to leave the guy with no money on him at all. But of more concern to me was his drunken state and I didn't want to just leave him here on his own. He looked really unsteady on his feet and Maybole High Street is a steep hill with big heavy lorries thundering up and down it. It's basically the main A77 road from Glasgow to Stranraer. I took Rab by the arm and we gently eased our way through a broad walkway towards the High Street and the cafe. Just then a youth about fifteen years old appeared round a corner into view. He seemed a nice enough lad and he headed straight for us. Rab and I stopped our tottering. He still held onto my arm.

Youth – Hi, Rab

Rab (recognising the lad) – Hi, young 'un

Youth (to me) – Who are you pal?

Me (touching my taxi driver badge) – I'm a taxi driver. I just brought Rab over from Dalmellington. He doesn't look too good on his feet, young 'un

Youth – Come on, Rab. I'll walk you

Rab – Aye, thanks, young 'un

Me – Tell Rab he can owe us the £18. He's only got a tenner on him

Youth – Aye, OK, pal

The young lad took Rab's arm and I let go. I watched them slowly walk away then I returned to my taxi, rolled a cigarette and lit up. This wasn't the first time I'd let someone owe us for a hire and Rab was regular enough for us not to worry about getting paid. I smoked my cigarette and idly gazed about at nothing in particular. Just then a voice broke my idleness.

Lady – You, Mr Taximan!

I turned and it was a lady with the young lad who'd taken Rab a few minutes earlier.

Me – Yes, madam

Lady – Did you bring a guy called Rab here in your taxi?

Me – Yes, I did. Is he OK?

Lady – Aye, he's OK. My boy here says that Rab owes you £18 for the taxi. Is that right?

The lady looked quite sternly at me. I thought that maybe she didn't believe the story.

Me – Yes, he does but it's OK. Rab can owe us and pay next time we see him. He's a good regular of ours

Lady – Here

She gave me a £20 note.

Lady (smiling) – No point Rab owing it you. He wouldn't remember it anyway so I'll pay you now. Keep the £2 change. Thanks for not just dumping him and driving off. My boy said you were holding Rab's arm. Thanks

Me – Pleasure. I'm just glad he's OK

So instead of having to explain to Boss that we were owed money, I made a tip and another satisfied customer. Didn't happen often so I savoured hires like that.

Banned – March 2010

There was a lady in the village who Boss banned from our taxis after a stream of incidents that thankfully never involved me. I drove her a few places in the taxi for the first few months I worked the day shift, then Boss announced she was on the banned list... for ever... with no chance of a reprieve ever. She was well and truly banned in other words. Most bans might be lifted after a period of time, but this lady was banned until the end of time plus a hundred years. She was also banned by Andy's taxis and a few other businesses too, I believe. Not just in Bellsbank and Dalmellington either. Businesses in neighbouring villages had also banned her.

She was a single lady in her fifties called Meg, and this one week I was covering the local parcel run in the village while Pete was off, and I noticed a parcel for Meg when I ran through the paperwork in the office before I did the round.

Me – Er, Boss

I pointed to the paperwork and Boss ambled over and peered at it.

Boss – Bollocks! OK deliver the parcel and if she gives you any nonsense whatsoever, just bring it back here. She ain't getting it

Me – OK Boss, no worries

So I set off and delivered all the parcels barring Meg's in about two hours. I had a quick cigarette by the shops then headed for

Meg's. I wasn't expecting anything to happen really other than maybe be on the receiving end of a scowling face. I never had any bother with the lady at all myself even though I found her to be quite disagreeable on my few encounters with her, and could easily see why she was banned from virtually everywhere. I walked to her door with clipboard under my arm and parcel in hand. I knocked on her door and it swiftly opened.

Me (being as formal and polite as possible) – Parcel for a Miss Soandso, madam

She didn't say a word and took the parcel off me and slung it back into her house with a look of total disdain.

Me – I just need you to sign here, madam, please

I passed her the clipboard and she signed it... but held on to it after she'd finished.

Meg – Tell your fuckin' boss...

Me (butting in) – Just give me the clipboard back please madam then I can be on my way

Meg (totally ignoring me) – ... he's ruined my life... blah, blah, blah

I mentally switched off listening to her, and stood about three yards away holding my hand out waiting for my clipboard.

Me – Meg, I'll just talk over you. I want the clipboard. Nothing else interests me. Give me the clipboard. I'll just keep talking and believe me I have actually talked the back legs off a small horse. A donkey if you like. Yes the hind legs. I have talked so much the government thought about...

Just then she threw the clipboard at me, and somehow its trajectory took it straight for my hand instead of my face which is where she probably aimed it. I caught it with barely any movement on my part and jammed it under my arm.

Me – Thank you, madam. I bid you good day

I reported back to Boss that there was no nonsense when I delivered Meg's parcel as I didn't see any point in raising his blood pressure over it.

A few months went by and a guy in the village, Karl, started his own one-man private hire business which he's perfectly entitled to do, and in short order Boss and myself learned that Meg had phoned Karl for a taxi, then proceeded to try and get him to do some household chores and other sundry nonsense. He promptly banned her. Neither Boss nor myself had any issues with Karl whatsoever, but we wanted to rib him about the Meg incident and I soon got my chance.

I was parked next to Karl one day shortly afterwards, and I shouted over to him while I pretended to have a phone call about a hire I couldn't do.

Me – Hey Karl!

Karl – Hiya, John... What's up, pal?

Me (pointing at my taxi mobile) – I can't do this hire and was wondering if you fancied it. Up to Glasgow

Karl – Sure, where from?

I told him Meg's address.

Karl (laughing) – Fuck off!

Volcano – April 2010

The volcano that erupted in Iceland in April 2010 sent a large cloud of ash into the atmosphere which drifted over most of Europe, and caused various problems for weeks afterwards. I noticed a light dusting of ash on my own car this one morning and thought, "Oh that'll be from that volcano." I arrived at work and noticed ash on the taxis and pretty much everything else too. It was everywhere and very noticeable.

Boss had taken someone to Glasgow and I was on my own for the next few hours until he returned. Mid-morning came and I took a call from Bev (of the Uruguay incident) and I soon picked her up at home to take her to the Co-op.

Me – Morning, Bev

Bev – Hi, John

Me – Co-op?

Bev – Aye

A bit further down the road I noticed a black car which seemed to have attracted more ash than most. Its roof and bonnet were covered in light grey ash.

Me – Look at that car, Bev

Bev – Which one?

Me (pointing) – That black one over there... See all that grey dust on it?

Bev – Aye. My husband's car had some on it this morning. What is it?

Me – Ash from that volcano. Wow, that was some eruption

Bev – Volcano?

Me – Yes... That one in Iceland

Bev – Iceland?

Me – Erupted the other day

Bev – No such thing

This statement shocked me a bit. For one horrible moment I had the feeling that Bev thought I'd made up the country of

Iceland, just like I'd made up Uruguay.

Me – Eh?

Bev – A volcano erupting... they're all dead aren't they? Dormant

Me – No, there's loads of them all over the place

Bev – What? That erupt?

Me – Well, yes... Iceland is a huge volcano anyway really

Bev – Really?

Me – Yes... Iceland is quite a volcano hotspot

Bev – And there are active volcanoes everywhere?

Me – Not everywhere... Lots in the Pacific... Hawaii... Italy has a few...

Bev – Italy?

Me – Yes, there's Etna... Stromboli I think... Dunno if Vesuvius still erupts but there's a few in Italy

Bev (looking a bit concerned) – None here though?

Me – In Britain? No... Edinburgh had one thousands of years ago, I think... Well, dormant now

Bev – Thank God for that, eh?

Me – Er… yes

So after this wee exchange, and I'd dropped Bev off at the Co-op, I took some more hires round and about over the next hour or so. Then Boss arrived back in the village and shouted me over the radio.

Boss – TC1 back in Dalmellington

Me – I'm on a hire just now for the next few minutes. Nothing else on

Boss – Roger. I'll go and make a brew at the office

Me – I'll be there myself shortly

I soon finished the hire I was on and returned to the office and walked in. Boss was in the wee kitchen out of sight to me making a coffee.

Me – Hi, Boss

Boss – Been busy?

Me – The usual. I had Bev in the taxi today though

Boss – Oh, aye

Me – I was telling her the dust on the cars was ash from that volcano

Boss – Aye

Me – She didn't realise that volcanoes still erupted

Boss's head appeared from round the kitchen door and he was chuckling.

Boss – I've got worse than that

Me – Hard to imagine but go on

Boss – I was telling that bloke I just took to Glasgow about the volcano and he said, "What's a volcano?"

Confusion – May 2010

I answered the phone around ten o'clock one morning and could see straight away it was Madge.

Me – Hello, T&C Taxis

Madge – Hi John... I need a taxi to the bank

Me – OK, Madge I'll be up in a few minutes

Madge – OK

Naturally I knew exactly where she lived, so I was soon on her drive around three minutes later. She scurried out her house and got in alone with no sign of her chap.

Me – Morning, Madge

Madge – Hi, John

Me – Where's Steve today?

Madge – Oh I sent him shopping

I liked a wee joke with my customers and I think Madge enjoyed banter more than most. She was a genuinely likeable lady, although very inattentive to either the world around her, or her own situation.

Me – So... Pulling a bank job, are we? I'll keep the motor running while you pull the blag, Madge. Get non-sequential notes only

Madge (laughing) – OK, John

Me – Even though we're gonna pull a bank job, Madge... Er... Seatbelt... Don't want the police lifting us, do we?

Madge (seriously) – Sorry, John

Watching Madge, or indeed a lot of folks, trying to put a seatbelt on was torture. They would pull on the handbrake, the side of the seat, their coats and everywhere else, while staring out the windscreen and talking. Eventually I belted Madge in like I did with a lot of my passengers.

After a brief and uneventful journey, we arrived at the bank.

Me – Do you want running to your brother's after? Or back home? Shops maybe?

Madge – Home

Me – I'll wait here then

Madge – OK

Madge would occasionally want taking to her brother's house on the other side of the village, but not on this occasion. I always asked because she, and others, would often fail to mention details like this and if I got a call from someone wanting a taxi in a few minutes' time, I'd know with better accuracy what time I could get to them. I prided myself on such preciseness.

She scurried over the road to the bank which, barring a yard or so, is directly opposite the Keystore shop where I'd parked. Madge scurried back from the cashpoint within two minutes.

Me – My word Madge, you're quick

Madge – Aye

Me – You don't want anything from the Keystore?

Madge – No

Me – OK, we're off

After another event-free drive, we were soon at Madge's and she handed me a £20 note.

Me – Anything smaller, Madge? It's less than £5

Madge – Er...

She rummaged in her purse and extracted a tenner. I sorted some change and she was soon out the car and scurrying back to the house, but quickly U-turned and headed back to the car. I wound my window down.

Madge – Ooh, John

Me – Yes, Madge

Madge – Can you do me a favour?

Me – I'll try... what is it?

Madge (handing me a £20 note) – Can you get me some messages from the Keystore?

Me – Certainly, Madge. I'll drop them round within the next twenty minutes or so

Unbelievably, Madge wanted messages from the very same shop we'd just been parked outside. I committed the items to memory, and I then drove off to a hire I had due in a few minutes. I completed that hire easily and swiftly enough then parked once more outside the Keystore to get Madge's messages. By the time I got the two items and drove back to Madge's I think about twenty minutes had elapsed.

On the short drive back to her house, I saw her boyfriend Steve walking to her house with the exact same items in a clear plastic bag. I got there first, gave Madge the messages and change, then pulled off the drive just as Steve arrived and we exchanged cheery waves.

The Good – May 2010

The busiest weekend of the year for us was the last weekend in May when there was a music festival at a remote farm about seven miles up the road, and music fans from all over the country and abroad descended on wee Dalmellington. I covered the festival every year and loved every hire I had and met some great people from all over the UK and beyond. They came from all over the globe but they often needed a taxi to make those final few miles.

The number 52 bus stopped at Dalmellington then returned to Ayr. Festival-goers would get off the bus after travelling from wherever and suddenly find they were seven miles short, unless of course they knew that already. From the village it was a few miles down the A713 towards Carsphairn, then along a farmer's drive, down the Scottish Power Board's access road, over a silly wee bridge and so on. Most of them had lots of heavy camping gear too.

Needless to say, many of them opted to use our taxis instead of a long trudge up the road and down the track. Most of the festival-goers usually arrived on Friday so that was the busiest day, and Saturday morning was hectic too. But by Saturday afternoon things started to ease off. Boss took the day off while I worked alone once things got quieter. I was stood outside the office when a couple of stoned festival-goers walked round to the office from the bus terminal in the square, then while I was trying to get some sense out of them, I got a desperate call from an American lass at the festival who wanted to return to Dalmellington sharpish.

Girl (in an American accent) – Hello... I need a private hire vehicle back to Dalmellington as soon as you can please

Me – You need a what? Oh yes right... Well you're in luck. I'm just about to bring some folk up. I'll be there in twenty minutes. What's your name?

Girl – Fleckner

Me – Twenty minutes then. Be at the ticket office by the dam. I haven't got time to hang about. I'll be in a silver saloon with blue door stickers

Girl – Hey, sure. No problems. We're at the ticket office already

Me – Excellent. Twenty minutes, OK?

Girl – OK

She was also the first and only person to ever ask for a "private hire vehicle" rather than a taxi in all the years I did the job. I finally got some sense out of the two I had with me and took them to the festival. They were an odd couple but after driving a cab for nearly four years at this point, nothing fazed me any more.

I pulled up at the ticket office by the dam, the couple paid me and trudged off the final one mile into the festival itself. We didn't drive past the dam because it was a one-way dirt track with no passing places and a drop down to a wee burn on one side. I drove down it once when I took a band right into the festival and nearly ripped the exhaust off the car, so after that we only went to the dam and no further. Within a minute of my arrival, a cleanly dressed young lass and an equally clean cut chap ran up to me.

Girl – Is this vehicle for Fleckner?

Me – Aye it is. Get in

Guy – Hey cheers, buddy, this is real swell of you

They were clean cut folk dressed way too smart for the festival I thought. Not like the usual festival-goers I'd taken there the past few years who were always dressed in "interesting" clothes, covered in soil and reeking of "substances". The drive to Dalmellington passed very agreeably. Then Guy spoke. I can't recall their first names.

Guy – Hey, buddy, can you take us to Edinburgh please?

Me (thinking the guy was joking) – Yes sure, mate

Guy – Hey man, I'm serious. By the time we've gotten the bus to Ayr, then the train up to Edinburgh, we'll waste too much time, and we're in kind of a rush

I now realised the guy was serious. Boss was at home and I couldn't just leave the village "unattended" as he would call it. I needed cover. The furthest hire I'd had to date was a guy to Dumfries about forty five miles away, but Ayr is about as far as I drove to normally which is just fifteen miles up the road. Edinburgh is around eighty miles.

Me – Er... I'll just phone my boss. But I'm sure it will be OK

Guy – That would be real swell

I pulled into the village instead of driving past it and parked up outside the office and phoned Boss.

Me – Hi Boss, I've got an American couple here I just picked up from the festival

Boss (sounding bored) – Yes... and

Me – Well, they want me to take them to Edinburgh

Boss (laughing) – Well, what the fuck you doing phoning me

you dafty cunt?

Me (laughing) – I can't leave the village unattended now can I Boss? Your rules remember?

Boss – Aye, you're right. Where are you now?

Me – Outside the office

Boss – I'll be down in two minutes

Me (to the Americans) – No worries. Boss will be down in a wee while to lift the phone off me, then we're away

Girl – Hey, this is really nice of you, buddy

Me – No worries

Boss parked up in front of me, we both got out our taxis and conversed between them. He had a wee peek in to look at the couple kissing and what-not on the back seat.

Boss – They don't look like festival-goers

Me – I think that's why they want home. Not their scene and had enough, I suspect

Boss flicked through the fare listings in his wee book and showed me the amount the hire would cost.

Boss – Get the fare off them first, then fill up the car, and phone me when you've dropped them off, or if you get stuck. I reckon it'll take you about two hours to Edinburgh

Me – Aye, will do

Boss lifted the phone off me, then drove off. Guy peeled off a wedge of tenners from a huge roll in his jacket and paid me. I filled up the taxi, then took them to Edinburgh and had one of the most pleasant and intellectual conversations in the taxi I'd ever had. He was doing a degree in politics and she was studying history, both at Edinburgh University. I enjoyed it that much, I didn't even mind the measly £2 tip.

He gave me directions once we got to Edinburgh, but after I'd dropped them off in the heart of the city, I had the task of navigating myself out of a place I'd never been to before, never mind drive in. I remember seeing on a map that Scotland's capital had a southern bypass road so I basically just headed south by following the sun. I soon saw a sign that said "Kilmarnock", followed that and arrived back in Dalmellington after the briefest visit anyone has probably ever paid to one of the finest cities in the country. I've been back to Edinburgh since for a wee holiday and it's a truly great city.

The Bad – May 2010

A few days after the previous story, the festival was over and I went into work on the Tuesday.

Boss – Follow me in your taxi. We're off to St John's of Dalry to pick up some folk for Prestwick Airport. It's a two-car jobby

Me – Will do

I remembered taking the phone call for this hire a week or so before. I also remember saying to the guy that I'd get Boss to call him back to obtain address details and confirm we could actually do the job. I took the guy's number and explained it all to Boss when I saw him later that day. Boss said something along the lines of, "Oh yeah, I ken where that is." As the following story will explain, I don't think he did.

I got in my cab and followed Boss down the A713 to St John's of Dalry which is miles the other way from Prestwick Airport, and looked forward to a fairly leisurely hire. How wrong can you be?

We got to St John's and Boss swung his car round and we headed back up the road we'd just come down. I thought, "What's gone wrong?" We turned up a driveway. Obviously we missed it on the way in. This drive was miles long with a gate halfway down it, so it just seemed to take forever to get to this place. We got to the house but no-one was in.

I sat in my taxi with the windows up and couldn't hear what Boss was prattling on about to himself. He made a phone call then we were off again back up the enormous drive to the main road. "Where is this place?" I thought. And Boss being Boss, wouldn't tell me anything as to what was going on. The radio remained silent. We drove a mile up the road, then turned up another driveway.

It was the worst driveway I'd ever seen. Huge potholes and sharp flinty rocks stuck out of it. I ground the bottom of the taxi a few times. Deep ditches both sides and sheep everywhere. It seemed to go on forever, but finally we got to a house... with no-one in except some workmen, and I saw them giving Boss directions and I could tell he wasn't happy. We turned round and headed on out ... and met a lady in a Volvo estate coming the other way just as we got to the bottom of this hilly bit of the narrow driveway. I could almost see steam coming out of Boss's ears.

There was a wee bit of grass that Boss managed to squeeze onto to let the Volvo past because she wouldn't reverse and make it easier for him, and he scraped the bottom of his taxi on the grass which turned black with dirt off the bottom of the car. I could also see that Boss's front right tyre looked a bit flat too. Must have been one of these dagger-like rocks. And instead of letting me onto this wee bit of blackened grass where there wasn't much of a ditch, she drove at me and forced me to reverse uphill, but I spied another wee bit of grass with no ditch and got on it double quick. I was fuming. Why she just didn't wait for a couple of seconds to let me get by I couldn't work out.

The Volvo pulled up next to me as I sat on the grass, and I could see Boss's taxi slowly limp towards the gate in the distance.

Volvo lady – Hello

Me (through gritted teeth) – Hi

Volvo lady – Can I help you?

Me – I'm just following my boss and I think we've got the wrong house so we'll be on our way. Sorry

Volvo lady – Oh I see... Your boss has got a puncture, I think. I heard him shouting

Me – Oh, has he? I'd better go help him

Volvo lady – OK, bye

Me – Bye

I caught up with Boss. He'd parked by the gate and got the jack and spare wheel out of the boot. Two dead sheep sat yards from where he'd stopped and they stunk to high heaven. There were flies everywhere.

Boss – Let's get this fuckin car up in the air and get this wheel changed, John

Me – Aye

As an ex tyre-fitter myself, I was confident that Boss and myself would have the job done in minutes. Boss started jacking while I cracked the nuts off. The jack started sinking in the drive and the taxi started rolling backwards. It just would, wouldn't it?

Boss – Fuck's sake! I'll keep jacking... just get your foot on that fuckin brake pedal.

Me – Aye

Boss jacked up the taxi, whipped the wheel off and the spare was on within seconds. I'd never pressed a brake pedal so hard in my life. Well... until the following story anyway. Panic over... Boss's mobile rang, and while I threw the flat tyre and jack back in his boot, he explained we'd had a puncture and would be there in a few minutes. We were off again. Boss thrashed the fuck out of his taxi but I kept up easily because my taxi was quicker. I never did understand why Boss preferred driving the estate to the larger engined saloon, but I benefited from that decision. A mile or so further and we turned into the third drive of the trip and there was a big family stood by the front door of their house with heaps of suitcases... Phew! Eventually.

A nice family, a jolly nice trip and we got them to the airport on time. Boss never did tell me why we went up two wrong driveways. I reckon he got lost or forgot the house name but knew roughly where it was, and was just guessing. He was like that.

The Ugly – July 2010

One quiet Sunday afternoon, I was relaxing on one of our taxi office's least lumpy and cluttered armchairs playing Gem Drop, while Boss attended to the seemingly endless sea of paperwork that running a private hire business generated. The phone rang and Boss briefly conversed with the caller. I heard Boss repeat the address for the pick-up, a name, and Patna as the destination while he glanced at me with a wee grimace on his face. He finished the call.

Boss – Right then, John. Pick this Charlie guy up and take him to Patna. He's a bit of a herbert so be fuckin' careful. OK? He might not like you because you're a Brummie or some such pish. Just be cool and... well, you've been doing this job long enough now

Me – Er, OK, Boss. I'll use my jovial witty banter to calm him down if he gets arsy

Boss – Just get him to Patna OK. He'll probably want the Wheatsheaf

Me – Aye, OK

I headed off to pick this guy up thinking just how bad can he be. I'd met some herberts already, and to be honest, even they were decent sorts once I got to know them. Even the local ankle bracelet lads, big tough old locals, junkies... you name it. None of them had ever given me an ounce of bother really. Sure, I had good natured banter about my Brummie accent and my constant mentioning of West Bromwich Albion, but never any actual violence apart from one rubbishy attempt at a punch which hit the taxi window.

I got to the pick-up address and a regular looking guy about the same age as myself stepped out and got in my taxi.

Me – Afternoon, sir. Patna, isn't it?

Charlie – Aye. The Wheatsheaf

Boss as usual was correct and I knew the Wheatsheaf pub so off I set. We were just about to leave the village, and would therefore lose radio contact with the office, when Charlie spoke.

Charlie – Oh, er... Can you take me to Ayr instead?

Me – I'll check... (then into the radio) TC6 to Control

Boss – Aye, go ahead TC6

Me – Charlie wants to go to Ayr now

Charlie – Just take me. Why do you have to ask?

Me – Well, I may have another hire in Dalmellington and have to get back for it

Charlie – Can't your fuckin' boss do it?

Me – Well, he might, but I like to keep him informed anyway. He'll expect me back in twenty minutes from Patna not one hour

Boss (radio) – Aye, that's fine TC6

Me (radio) – Roger, Control. See you in one hour

Charlie (angrily) – Aye, what was so difficult about that?

Me (thinking "here we go") – Nothing, sir

A few miles passed.

Charlie – How much is it to Ayr?

Me – £18, sir

He handed me a £20 note and told me to keep the change. We carried on down the A713, past Patna and soon neared the roundabout where it met the A77 Ayr bypass at the Queen Margaret Academy. Charlie had been asleep the past few miles which was a relief to be honest. He seemed a bit grumpy and aggressive, yet he'd given me a £2 tip. I woke him up.

Me – Sir, we're near Ayr now. Which part of town you want?

Charlie – You ken that estate opposite Queen Margaret Academy?

Me – I do

Charlie – There. I'll direct you. I don't ken the actual address

Me – OK

He wanted an estate in the east of Ayr not far off where we were, and I soon turned into Kincaidston Drive and pootled along at about ten m.p.h waiting for some directional pointing from Charlie. After a while we'd done a few hundred yards while Charlie looked all around as we crawled along.

Charlie (aggressively) – Nah! This is no fuckin' good! Tell you what. Take me to Dalmilling

Me – The north end of town?

Charlie – Aye

Me – OK, sir

Dalmilling was a district in the north of Ayr that I got mixed up with the village of Dalmellington when I first moved to the area, but that earlier confusion meant I knew exactly where it was now. I swung the car round gently and headed out of the estate for Dalmilling a few miles away. I wanted this hire over with as soon as possible. Charlie was getting very angry. I was just about to turn left out of Kincaidston Drive to head for Dalmilling through Ayr itself, rather than turn right and then north on the A77 bypass, when Charlie piped up again.

Charlie – Patna!

Me – You want back to Patna now sir?

Charlie – Aye

I then needed to turn right to get back to Patna, not left.

Charlie (very aggressively) – Turn fuckin' left here, big 'un!

Me – Patna is back that way, sir

I pointed to my right as we neared the junction.

Charlie – I want to go to fuckin' Main Road

Me – Main Street, Patna, sir?

Charlie (fuming) – No, for fuck's sake! Main fuckin' Road, fuckin' Ayr, not fuckin' Patna!

Me – Up Dalmilling way?

Charlie – Yes up fuckin' Dalmilling way!

I knew exactly where Main Road, Ayr was. It ran past Dalmilling. The few parcel rounds I'd done in Ayr the previous few years had given me quite a good knowledge of certain roads in Ayr and Prestwick, and Main Road was one of them. There was a Main Street back in Patna and he clearly didn't want that. I wanted this guy out the taxi right there and then. I was absolutely fuming inside as I turned left back onto the A713 into Ayr.

Me (trying to calm the situation) – I'm very sorry, sir but I got mixed up there. My apologies

Charlie – Tell you what, pal. Take me to fuckin' Patna

Me – But, sir I thought you wanted Main Road up Dalmilling way?

Charlie – No. Don't come the cunt with me, big 'un

I'd had enough. It was obvious to me that he had decided to be deliberately awkward and would continue to keep changing his mind depending on which direction I was facing. Patna was eight miles back but I knew somewhere a mile or so away that I'd take Charlie instead. The sooner he was out my cab the better.

Me – Ooh, I know where I can take you

Charlie – Where?

Me – The junction of John and Allison Street in Ayr

Charlie – What's there?

Me (firmly and staring at him) – The fuckin' police station

Charlie (very aggressively and loudly) – You do that and I'll punch...

He never got to say the words "your head in" because I'd decided in the last few seconds that this hire was ending. I already didn't have my seatbelt on which taxi and PHV drivers are allowed to do, and Charlie hadn't put his seatbelt on since I picked him up either. His choice. In a matter of milliseconds I'd checked my rear view mirror and slammed the brakes on as hard as I'd ever done in my life.

Charlie shot forward and smashed into the dashboard, while I braced my arms rigid on the steering wheel. Ignition key out and handbrake on, then I was out the car in a few more milliseconds. I bounded over the deserted street, whipped out my phone and called the police. I could see Charlie stirring in the car as he picked himself up and rubbed his head.

After a quick call with Strathclyde Police, I lit a cigarette and just waited. Charlie got out the car still rubbing his head and after a wee while he shouted over to me.

Charlie – Come on, big 'un. What's going on?

Me – Nothing, sir. I need a fag

Charlie – Come on to fuck man and get me home, ya cunt

Me – Nah, it's OK, sir, thanks. I need a fag and had to make an urgent phone call. Give me a minute

A police van arrived in amazingly short order and parked directly in front of my taxi. A burly cop got out and shouted over to me.

Cop – You OK, sir?

Me – Aye, I'm OK

Cop (pointing at my taxi) – Is that the guy in your taxi?

Me – Aye, it is

Cop – Has he paid you for the hire?

Me – Aye. And a wee tip to be honest

Cop – Leave this to us, sir

Another cop got out the police van and they took Charlie away. I never heard any more from the police. I phoned Boss, explained what had occurred and drove back to the village. I never saw Charlie again, but he didn't live in the village Boss told me. He was visiting friends and lived miles away although he came from the area originally.

Dildo – August 2010

Natalie sent me one Saturday morning to pick up Sharon who used us pretty regularly. Her and her mate Jane needed picking up after a boozy party and taking home. I got to the pick-up address and Sharon came out with the usual smeared make-up and hardly anything on. She got in the front seat.

Sharon – Hi, John

Me – Hi, Sharon... Good party, was it?

Sharon (laughing) – Aye... Me and Jane have been to a naughty party

Me – Oh... sounds like fun

Sharon – Oh, it was... It was... te, he, he

Jane came out the house now, with slightly less make-up smearage and got in the back. I moved off and headed to Sharon's house.

Jane – Hi, John

Me – Hi, Jane... Sharon says you've been at a naughty party

Jane – Aye... te, he, he

Me – So what goes on at these naughty parties then?

Sharon – This!

She pulled out a huge purple dildo from her bag and waved it in my face.

Me – Ooh, a dildo... So where's that been then?

Sharon – Nowhere… Yet... te, he, he

Me – OK, so where is it going then?

Jane – Up the first bloke we can find!... te, he, he

Me – Nice

Well they didn't stick it up me in case you're wondering, but I wonder if they did stick it up the first bloke they found? Maybe they went to the party in the following story.

We're The Fuckin Best – September 2010

I got a call from a young lad called Bazza this one Saturday late afternoon. He was at Diane's house. I was approaching the end of the street he was in when he phoned so I swung into the road without bothering to ask where he wanted to go. It would be local and I had nothing else due. He got in and sat in the front, and Diane was tagging along too and sat right in the middle of the back seat. Diane was a lady who swore like a builder, or maybe even a mild mannered taxi driver, and hated everything and everyone it seemed. Diane and Bazza weren't "together" either.

Me – Hi, Bazza. Hi, Diane... Where we off to?

Bazza – Seventeen Soandso Avenue... A party

Me – Ooh, party eh... Any nice ladies there?

Bazza – Nah, not my sort anyway

Me – Ooh!

Diane leaned forward and shouted very loudly in Bazza's ear.

Diane – Never mind "your fuckin' sort," ya wee cunt... Bellsbank lassies are the best... Best at fighting and we're the best at fuckin' shagging as well!

Me – Can't argue with that, Bazza

Bazza (unconvinced) – Aye

I often wonder how that party panned out.

What Fuckin' Law? – October 2010

I was sat in my taxi outside the office playing Gem Drop for a change this one day and not really paying much attention to the outside world. If folk wanted me they would sometimes just walk up to the car and get in to be honest. It was one of those days where it had been quiet all day and I'd just parked outside the office until the phone rang. I glanced up for some reason, and this guy was about twenty yards in front, on the pavement, with two walking sticks and he waved one of them at me. I started the car and pulled forward, stopping right next to him. He opened the door and leant in.

Him – Can you take me up to Suchandsuch Street please, pal? I've hurt my foot and I'm in agony here

Me – Sure... Get in, sir... Need a hand?

Him – No, I'm all right, pal

He struggled in with his two sticks. A big lummox of a bloke like myself with a bit of a belly. Forty years old, maybe. After he finally struggled in with his sticks and bags we were ready for the off. Unlike ninety nine percent of my passengers though, I didn't know his name.

Me – I need a surname please, sir

Him – Eh... what for?

Me – It's the law

Him – What fuckin' law?

I just thought, "here we go."

Me – 1982 Scottish Local Government Act

Him (astonished) – I've never fuckin' heard of this

Me – Stupid law I know, but there you go

Him – I'll get out then and get that fuckin' taxi over there

He pointed to one of Andy's guys parked further up the street.

Me – He'll want your name as well, sir... It's the stupid law you see

Him – I've had taxis before loads of times and never had to give my name

Me – Yes, well in a taxi you don't have to give your name... This is a private hire vehicle.... Not a taxi... The law is different... An idiotic and confusing law I agree, sir... I shouldn't even pick you up off the street...

Him (butting in) – Get your fuckin' boss on the radio now and...

Me (butting in firmly) – Boss isn't on duty... only me.... if you're not happy... get out

There was a tense pause while I hovered my pen over the clipboard ready to write his name in.

Him – I play for Stirling Albion and I hurt my foot and... come on, pal

Me – Stirling Albion eh, not West Bromwich Albion?... I still need a name... ANY name... I won't be asking for ID to prove your name... I just need a name, sir. I could be a really awkward sausage and ask you to phone up, which is what you're supposed to do. Not just waltz up or wave at me. I'm not that petty though. Asking someone to phone up when I'm sat here with the phone in my pocket would be even more idiotic than the stupid law which wants us to do that in the first place. But, and it's an important "but"... I need a name. You will give me a name otherwise I will apply my handbrake, switch the ignition off and return to a spot of Gem Drop. Are we clear?

Him – Anderson

Me – OK, we're off then, sir

I wrote Anderson on the booking sheet and tossed the clipboard back onto the dash and moved off. We got to the square a few yards from where I'd picked the guy up.

Anderson – Where's the bookies in this place, pal?

Me (pointing) – See that door where that guy in the white shirt is?

Anderson – Aye

Me – Bookies

Anderson (pointing at the Spar) – OK... can we stop at that shop down there?

Me – Aye

I pulled up outside the Spar and he got out, and I thought to myself, "Who is this guy? Never seen him in the village before ever."

He emerged from the shop a few minutes later chatting with a local character named Danny. Now I was a bit confused. He didn't know where the bookies was (which although it looks like a house rather than a shop, everyone in the village knows it's the bookies) which says to me he's not local... I've never seen him before which also says he's not local... But he seems to know Danny... Must be a relative or something. After a hearty series of goodbyes with Danny, Mr Anderson got back in the taxi with a couple of bags of messages.

Anderson (pointing to Danny) – Who's that guy?

Me – Danny... a local character

Anderson – He's cool... great guy

Me – Yes, Danny's a great guy... lives in your street, too

I drove off and headed for Suchandsuch Street.

Anderson – Yeah, when you asked for my name I thought you were the police

Me – And why would I be the police, Mr Anderson? This isn't a cop car

Anderson – I'm just out the jail... six years I did

Me – Oh, I see

Anderson – So I thought it was a trap

Me – A trap for what exactly Mr Anderson?

I talked a lot of pish about this and that so he couldn't talk any more. I got him home, carried his messages up to his door, gave him one of our business cards, and he paid me.

Me – OK, Mr Anderson. See you around

Anderson – The name's not really Mr Anderson... it's Mr Stevens

Me – Like I said earlier Mr Stevens... I need a name... not necessarily yours... know what I mean?

Stevens/Anderson – Hey, you're all right, you are! Cheers, pal

Me – Bye

I called in at Boss's house on the way back to the office and we had a wee chat. Within a few hours Boss had obtained, through a source, all of Mr Stevens's details and everything bar his inside leg measurement.

The Runner – December 2010

Over the years, I came to experience many different goings on, in and around the taxi. Violence, abuse, bodily fluids, sexual references and so on. The one aspect of taxi driving I'd never had was "a runner". i.e. someone running off without paying. I reckoned that in a wee village like Dalmellington it was probably unlikely to happen compared to the anonymity of a town or big city. Perversely enough I always wanted someone to do a runner. Like a badge of honour.

One day coming up to Christmas 2010, I was sat in my cab at the office, when four youths approached me. I knew them and had taken them various places over the years with never any bother. One of them was a bit of a herbert, but the other three were sound enough. I was actually just about to start the car and drive up to Bellsbank shops for a hire when they appeared and knocked on my window.

Lad 1 – Taxi up to Bellsbank, big 'un?

Me – Aye, get in lads

They all climbed in while I filled out the booking sheet, and off we went. Knowing virtually everyone's name is actually part of the problem in some ways. We won't ask their name when they book a private hire because we already know their name. Therefore folk don't think they're giving a name, like in a taxi, but I knew all four of them.

Lad 1 – How much is it, big 'un?

Me – £2.40p, bud

They proceeded to argue with each other about who was going to pay and all the usual carry on. The three in the back seat did a lot of whispering and sniggering while occasionally voicing their lack of money. As I drove up the brae to the estate, I decided to get a more definite destination than the general area of Bellsbank.

Me – Where in Bellsbank, lads?

Lad 1 – Oh er... shops. The shops, big 'un

Lad 2 – Aye, the shops, pal

Me – OK, lads. Shops it is

There was a wee row of shops on Merrick Drive, and I thought, "Ooh, what a stroke of luck. Exactly where I'm going anyway." I pulled into the wee parking bay outside Nicedays.

Me – That's £2.40p please, lads

Lad 1 (pointing to one of the lads in the back) – Oh, he'll get it

Lad 2 (pointing to another lad in the back) – Fuck off, I paid last time. He's paying

Lad 3 (getting out the car) – Am I fuck. You should fuckin' pay, ya cunt

Lad 4 was already running off down the street, and I knew then that I'd had my first, and only, runner pulled on me. Within seconds they were all out the car dashing up the street. I actually didn't bat an eyelid. I thought, "Ooh, a runner. Wow!"

I sat in the taxi and waited for my next hire. I crossed the details off the booking sheet and explained to Boss later that someone cancelled a hire they only booked minutes previously. I didn't see much I could actually do about it, so I played a bit of Gem Drop until the hire I was collecting showed up, and chalked the incident up to experience.

Apple Crumble – March 2011

During the daytime, once the school kid runs were out the way, it was mainly a case of ferrying senior ladies and gents about the village. Gents might go to their favourite boozer, while ladies may meet at the church hall for coffee mornings or visit friends and such like. I got to know a lot of them over the years, and often ran errands, did wee D-I-Y jobs, topped up electricity and gas cards, brought dustbins back from the roadside and all manner of things. I also always carried shopping bags for anyone, not just the senior ladies.

I carried some bulky shopping bags to Morag's front door this one day and noticed a broken bottle by her doorstep. I placed her messages on her kitchen counter.

Me – Morag, have you got a dustpan and brush? There's some glass by your doorstep. I was going to clear it up

Morag – Oh that's good of you, John

She found a wee brush and pan and I swept up the mess, wrapped it in a few bags and an old newspaper, and placed it in her bin. She thanked me, and off I went thinking no more of it.

Well, the next time I ran her home after a church meeting she asked me not to go once I'd escorted her to the door. She was unsteady on her feet and I always walked her to the door as I did with a lot of folks. I waited outside thinking nothing of it. She returned with a dish covered in a tea towel.

Morag – For you John, because you're so nice to me

Me – Oh. Wow thanks.

It was the nicest apple crumble I'd ever had, and it was moments like that which made the job, with all its perils and suchlike, worthwhile.

40,001 – May 2011

One sunny Sunday not long before I finished driving taxis for a living, I took a regular of ours, Carol, and her husband Mack down to Ayr. We swept along the traffic-free A713 and I noticed the Moon just above the horizon and directly ahead at certain times depending on the bends in the road. Carol was sat next to me while Mack took a back seat.

Me – Ooh, look at the Moon, Carol. Lovely, isn't it? In the daytime as well. Nice

Carol – Aye, it is

I love chatting with people, and I'd talk about anything rather than sit in a silent taxi. Maybe I shouldn't though.

Me – How far away do you think the Moon is Carol?

Carol (quickly) – Forty thousand miles

Me (nodding) – Hey, not bad. It's about two hundred and forty thousand miles but yours is a very good guess. I asked a guy once and he said eight miles

Carol – Eight miles?

Me – Yes, he said eight miles. I told him that's a ridiculously low figure and he then said it was ten miles

Carol – Ten miles?

Me – Yes. At least your guess was a bit more realistic

Carol – He must be a bit of an idiot, John

Me – So how far away do you think the Sun is?

Carol – Wow, the Sun eh?

Mack – Come on, love, you can do this

Carol – Forty thousand miles

Me – It's further than the Moon, Carol

Carol – Oh is it? Er, forty thousand miles then

Mack – Love, the Moon is two hundred and forty thousand miles away and the Sun is further

A wee pause.

Carol – I can't think of a bigger number than forty thousand

Mack – Bloody hell, love. Forty thousand and one would qualify

Carol – Sorry

Me – Och, no need to be sorry. Me asking stupid questions. The Sun is ninety three million miles away anyway

Carol – Wow, that's a long way

Me – Aye, it would cost a few quid in a taxi

I quickly changed the subject to *King Kong* which had been on TV a few nights before. It was a film I knew Carol liked and

made for a much easier line of conversation for the remaining
miles of the journey.